OBJECT-ORIENTED SYSTEMS IN C++

OBJECT-ORIENTED SYSTEMS IN C++

By

Dr. DURGESH PANT
Reader and Head, Department of Computer Science
S.S.J. Campus, Kumaun University
Almora (Uttaranchal)

MAHESH KUMAR SHARMA
Senior Lecturer
Department of Computer Science
Amrapali Group of Institutes, Haldwani
Uttaranchal

K.S. VAISLA
Reader
Kumaun Engineering College
Dwarahaat
Uttaranchal

FIREWALL MEDIA
(An Imprint of Laxmi Publications Pvt.Ltd.)
An ISO 9001:2015 Company
BENGALURU • CHENNAI • GUWAHATI • HYDERABAD • JALANDHAR
KOCHI • KOLKATA • LUCKNOW • MUMBAI • RANCHI •
NEW DELHI

OBJECT ORIENTED SYSTEMS IN C++

Printed and bound in India
First Edition : 2009, Reprint : 2011, 2013, 2014, 2016, 2017 Edition : 2018
ISBN 978-81-318-0250-2

Branches

✆	Bengaluru	080-26 75 69 30	
✆	Chennai	044-24 34 47 26,	24 35 95 07
✆	Guwahati	0361-254 36 69,	251 38 81
✆	Hyderabad	040-27 55 53 83,	27 55 53 93
✆	Jalandhar	0181-222 12 72	
✆	Kochi	0484-237 70 04,	405 13 03
✆	Kolkata	033-22 27 43 84	
✆	Lucknow	0522-220 99 16	
✆	Mumbai	022-24 93 12 61,	
✆	Ranchi	0651-220 44 64	

Published in India by

FIREWALL MEDIA
(An Imprint of Laxmi Publications Pvt.Ltd.)

An ISO 9001:2015 Company
113, GOLDEN HOUSE, DARYAGANJ,
NEW DELHI - 110002, INDIA
Telephone : 91-11-4353 2500, 4353 2501
Fax : 91-11-2325 2572, 4353 2528
www.laxmipublications.com info@laxmipublications.com

C—
Printed at:

CONTENTS

PART A: OBJECT-ORIENTED SYSTEMS

Chapters *Pages*

Chapters *Pages*

Chapters *Pages*

PREFACE

This book covers the syllabus of paper **"Object-Oriented System in C++"** of UP Technical and Uttaranchal Technical University. Students of other Indian universities can also read this as a text book. It teaches how to design and develop a real world system using object-oriented modeling concepts and later on how to write a program in C++ and how to properly use its features in computer programs. This book start with a concise introductory text on object-oriented methodologies, free from complex definitions, so that beginners can develop a good understanding of OOAD and use of e C++ language to implement it, in a short period of time.

Further in all chapters we combine a tutorial style based explanation of OOAD and C++ concepts through examples with a reference style. As a result, each chapter consists of relatively short sections pages that simplifies the students task.

The authors avoided to present an absolutely complete description of C++, while no important topic has been omitted, descriptions of some of the important topics like templates and exception handlings have been added for the sake of beginner students with easy examples. Questions of last year papers are also given in self review questions to prepare yourself for university examinations.

The book is primarily designed for use in undergraduate and postgraduate computer science courses having self review questions after each chapter . Without sit on computer and write program one can not learn C++ so we attached several lab exercises with small C++ projects. Book will be equally useful to professional programmers who intend to learn the language on their own.

This book is a result of 10 years queries and answers have been discussed by our dear students, you all are welcome to send your feedback for more improvement in future.

—Authors

ACKNOWLEDGEMENTS

During the course of writing this book, we had long discussions with many savants of the field on several topics, issues, they all deserve our sincere thanks. Without their pragmatic professional tips this book would not have seen the light of day. To name a few and mention some of their contributions:

The Hon'ble Vice Chancellor of Kumaun University Prof. C.P. Barthwal , an academic of international repute, has been the guiding force in our endeavour.

There has been a galaxy of experts of informatics and computer science who have been instrumental in bringing out this volume. We sincerely thank Prof. M. M. Pant, Dr. R. K. Dutta, Prof. P. S. Grover, Dr. D.K. Joshi, Prof. M.M.S Rauthan, Dr. Harish Kumar, Prof. Dharminder Kumar, Prof. R.K. Sharma, Dr. M.P. Thapalyal, Dr. K.S. Bhatia, Dr. Alok Kumar, Dr. Pradosh Kumar Sharma.

We thank from our core of heart to Sh. Chanan Lal Dhingra, Chairman, Sh R.C. Monga Vice Chairman, Mr. Sanjay Dhingra, CEO, Mr. Narendra Dhingra, Secretary, Amrapali Group of Institutes for his endless encouragement, Prof. K.K Pande, Director Amrapali Institute, for their suggestions and guidance and specially for their encouragement and support to write this book. Mr. K.K. Motla, Dr. Shishir Kumar, Mr. Prashant Rajput and Mr. Sandeep Budhani for their discerning comments and invaluable support.

At last many-many thanks to our lovable students whose queries and support in class gave us encouragement to write this book.

Without extended our heartly thanks to our family members Dr. Reema Pant, Chiya Pant, Vandana, Vama and Suhani sharma, Sujata, Toyesh and Bittu Vaisla for their love and support we can not end this acknowledgement.

Authors

FOREWORD

Although there are numerous books in the subject, it is a delight to see a fresh effort, by relative young faculty, who has tried to put together their experience in the context of learners in many Institutes, which are away from the National Spotlight.

I appreciate the enthusiasm of the authors, and their considerable efforts in putting together this book.

This is a well written book using Object - Oriented approach, to describe the methodology for developing not only small programs but software projects also using C++ as an Object - Oriented language. In this book theories and concepts are supported by appropriate programs and examples. The language of book is lucid and easy for a beginner student. Detailed chapters are in book to teach the students and software professionals, moving from OOP concepts to actual C++ source codes.

I am sure the book will be useful as supplementary text to those studying in the Open University System, as well as a basic text to be adopted by standard courses in various universities on the subject.

October 18th, 2006

Prof. M M Pant
E - 57, Greenwoods City
Sector 46,
Gurgaon - 122001
Haryana, India

Mobile:
+ 91-98 100 73724

E-mail:
Professor@MMPant.org

Website:
www.MMPant.org

M.M. Pant
Former Pro-Vice Chancellor
Indira Gandhi National Open University
Delhi

Dedicated

to

Our

Parents

Part - A

OBJECT-ORIENTED SYSTEMS

Chapter 1

OBJECT MODELING

1.1 THREE TYPES OF MODELING

To design, develop and describe the Object-oriented system and classes, we have three types of models:

1. Object model
2. Dynamic model
3. Functional model

The **object model** provides a static or structural point of view to describe the system, classes, and relationships. The **dynamic model** provides a stimulus response time based point of view to describe events, messages, and states. The **functional model** provides a transformation point of view to describe the transformation or changes of inputs to outputs. To model and prototype a system, there is a need to create diagrams, text specifications, and code in three general models shown above. These models group and organize the diagrams, text specifications, and code. First, the system models have information on the system as a whole, such as the system requirements and system drawing. We model the system from the three points of view: object view, dynamic view, and functional view.

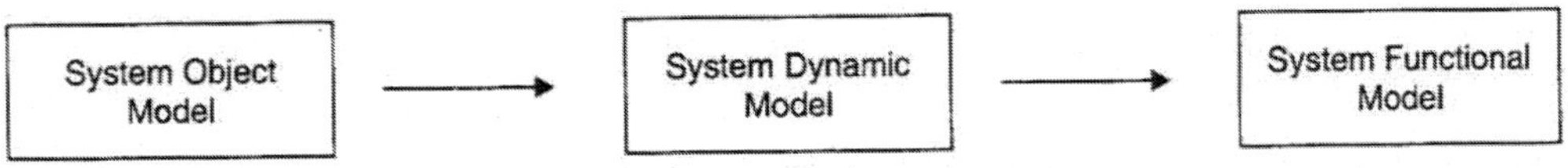

Next, you have to model classes, objects, and relationships in the system. For that you will create class diagrams and class specifications for classes within the system. In that phase you will model classes, objects, and relationships from the three points of view: object view, dynamic view, and functional view.

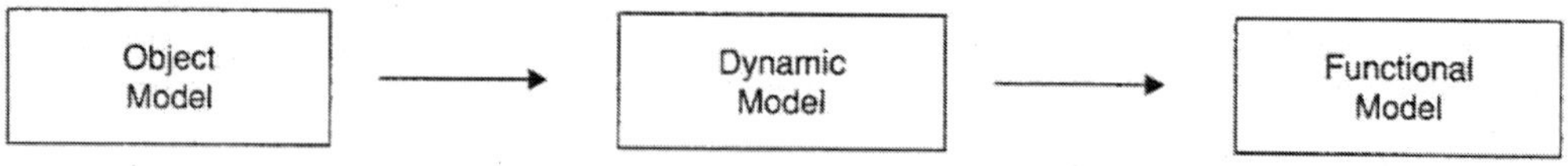

1.2 BASIC OBJECT-ORIENTED ENTITIES AND CONNECTIONS

There are three major entities in Object-oriented modeling are system, class, and object as given below:

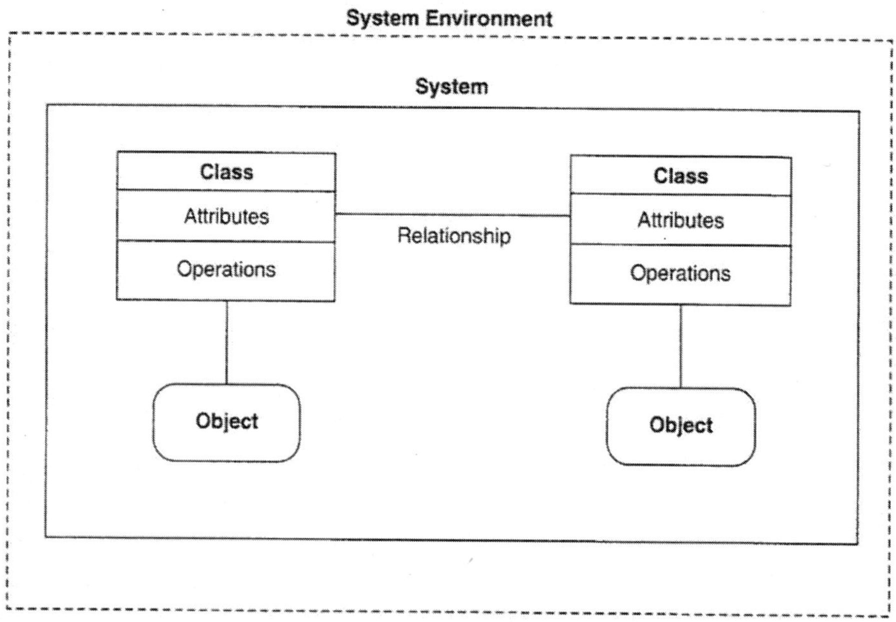

FIGURE 1.1 **Major Entities in O-O Modeling**

1.3 SYSTEM

A **system** is an entity that can be treated as a unit. A system is composed of simpler components that work together to perform a function. The term system is a general term that may refer to a very large system with smaller subsystems or to a small system without subsystems. A small system (or subsystem) consists of classes and objects that work together as a unit. A system may consist of 10 to 100 classes as a rough order of magnitude. A system interacts with other systems in a **system environment**. In C++ a **project** groups together a set of classes as a system. For execution, a system is an executable program (.EXE file), a dynamic link library, a process, or other executable entity. We model a system with a class diagram showing all the classes in the system. In this tutorial we will use the term system to refer to either a small system or to a subsystem. A sample system in this tutorial is the TV Control System which consists of approximately 15 classes in a single executable program.

1.4 CLASS

A **class** is a description of a group of objects with similar attributes, common operations, common relationships (association, aggregation, interaction, and generalization specialization) and a common semantic purpose. In software a class is a module. An **attribute** is a characteristic or property of an object. An attribute typically holds an atomic object, *e.g.*, an integer, a float, a character, etc. For example, an attribute of a car is gasQuantity which is a float. However, an attribute can hold a structured object or collection object to implement a relationship. For example, an attribute of a car could be currentPassengers which holds a set of current passenger objects. An attribute can hold a set of literals, *e.g.*, a string of characters. An **operation** is a function, action or set of actions. For example, an operation of a car is to "set gas quantity" and "start". A **relationship** is a connection or link between classes or between objects. The primary relationships are association ("has a"), aggregation ("part of"), generalization specialization ("is a"), and interaction ("calls or communicates"). For example, the Car Class has an association relationship with the Passenger Class. The Car Class has a generalization specialization relationship with the Vehicle Class. The Car Class has an aggregation relationship with the Motor Class. An interaction relationship (messages) exists between objects of the Car Class and objects of the Motor Class. The semantic purpose of a class is the reason for being or existence of objects of the class. For example, the semantic purpose of objects of the Car Class is to provide transportation to carry users from one location to another. We model a class with a class diagram and a class specification.

1.5 OBJECT

An **object** is an instance of a class. An object has an object name (ID) and a value for all attributes and associated objects. For example an object is Car11 with the attribute value of gasQuantity of 14.2 gallons. In execution an object responds to messages. We model objects in message scenarios. There are three major forms of objects:

- An **atomic object** is an object of a primitive class or data type, *e.g.*, integer, float, and character. Sample atomic objects are 1, 4.2, and 'a'.
- A **structured object** is an object of a class with attributes, operations, and relationships. Sample structured objects are car1, student3, and window2. For example, student1 = <age = 17, height = 5.9>.
- A **collection object** is an object of a collection, *e.g.*, array, list, set, and bag. A collection holds members. Sample collection objects are listOfStudents and setOfCourses. For example, listOfStudents = {student1, student2}.

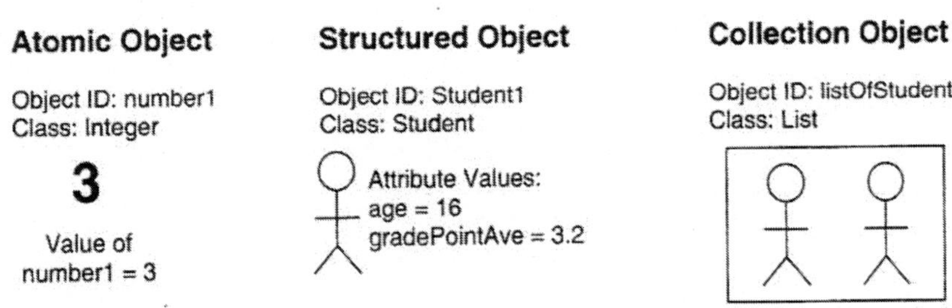

FIGURE 1.2 **Atomic, Structured, and Collection Objects**

1.6 LINK OR RELATIONSHIP

A Link or relationship is a link or connection between two classes or between two objects. There are four major Object oriented relationships:

1. Association
2. Aggregation
3. Generalization / specialization
4. Interaction / communication

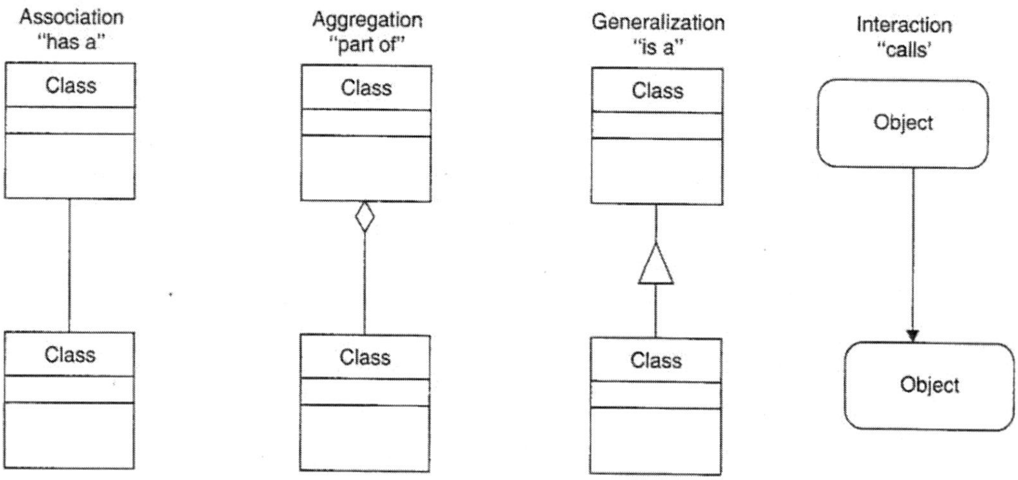

FIGURE 1.3 **Relationships in O-O Modeling**

Examples of Relationships

- A driver "has a" car. Association
- The Mobile "has a part" a screen. Aggregation
- The peacock car "is a" bird. Generalization specialization
- A customer "interacts" with a ATM machine. Interaction
- A classroom "has" furniture. Association
- A computer "has a part" hard disk. Aggregation
- A institute "is a" physical structure. Generalization specialization
- An student "interacts" with a faculty Interaction

Showing Relationships in Class Diagrams

The **class diagram** is a graphic representation of classes and relationships. Using the Rumbaugh OMT notation you can show association (has a), aggregation (part of) relationship, and generalization specialization (is a) relationships in a class diagram. Using class diagram you can show major relationships and cardinalities of generalization specialization like Vehicle to Car, 1 to 1 aggregation (Car to Motor), 1 to many aggregation (Car to Tire), 1 to zero or one association (Car to CellularPhone), and 1 to many association (Car to Passenger).

1.6.1 Association

Association setup a link between classes or it can be define a general mapping between the classes. An association relationship may be described as "has a", "associated with", or "knows about". For example a students "has a" computer, cellular phone or rollno. An association has a cardinality or multiplicity. This is the number of objects on one side of an association that may be associated with an object on the other side of the association. For example, if one students has one computer, this is an example of a 1 to 1 association. If a students has many cellular phones, then there is a 1 to many association between students and cell phone. The association symbol is a solid line between classes with the cardinality shown on each end of the solid line.

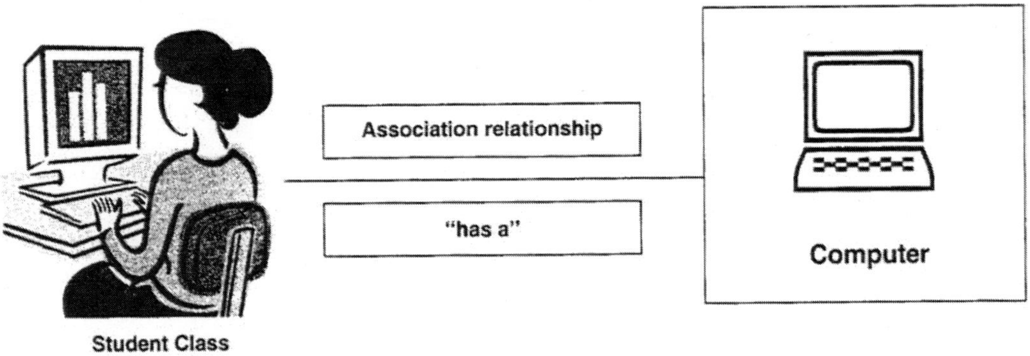

FIGURE 1.4(a) **Association Relationship**

Identifying Associations

You can identify association by looking for logical links or connections between two or more objects. One object may have knowledge about another object. For example, a institute "knows about" its students or employees. One object may "depend upon" another object. For example, a bank "depends upon" its customers, employees. Often it is useful to design drawing of the key objects in the system and show the association between the objects using that drawing.

The following are suggested steps to identify association relationships:

- Make a drawing or physical representation, *e.g.*, a car, a motor, a passenger.
- Identify the objects and their classes, *e.g.*, a car, a motor, a passenger.
- For each object, identify association relationships with the question "For each object what will be the associated objects?"
- Identify the multiplicity of each association relationship with the questions. "Is your object is associated with zero, one or many of the other object?" and "This association is either optional or required?"
- Identify if the relationship is an association ("has a") or an aggregation ("part of"). When you have some doubt always assume association ("has a").
- For each relationship, identify the constraints (limitations or rules).
- If available, check messages between objects in the dynamic model because messages indicate association and aggregation relationships.
- Create a class diagram, data dictionary, class specification, and prototype.

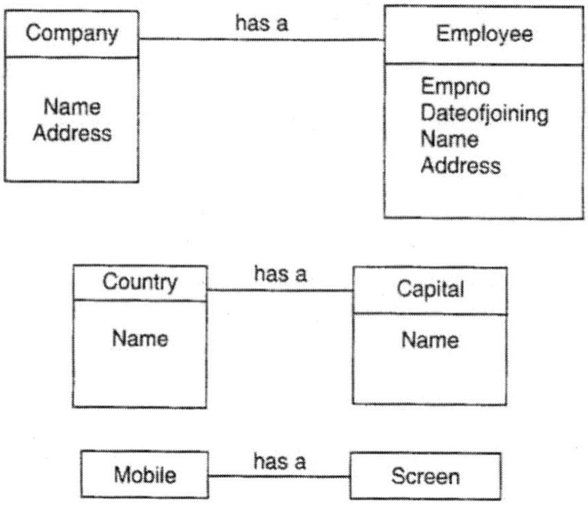

FIGURE 1.4(b) **Class Diagram Showing Relationships**

1.6.2 Aggregation

Aggregation used to setup a link between classes that has an association in form of "part of" a class. An aggregation relationship may be described as "part of" between an assembly (whole) object and part of objects. For example, a car "has a part" motor. A part object is an intrinsic part of an assembly object. When an assembly object is created, copied, or deleted, then the part object is created, copied or deleted. An aggregation relationship has a cardinality or multiplicity. This is the number of objects on one side of an aggregation that may be associated with an object on the other side of the aggregation. For example, a car has one motor. This is an example of a 1 to 1 aggregation. The aggregation symbol is a diamond with a solid line between classes with the cardinality shown on each end of the solid line.

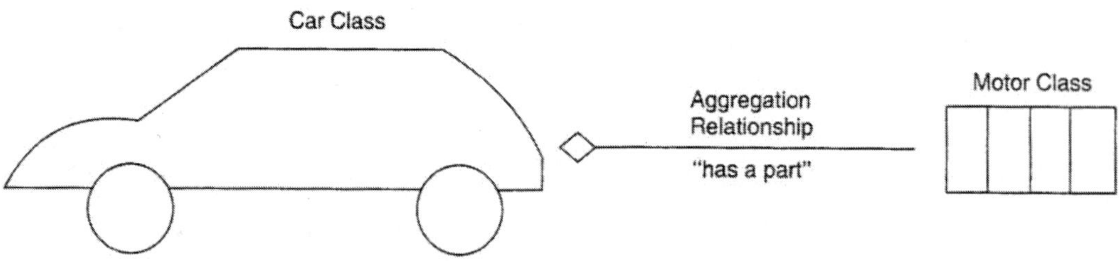

FIGURE 1.5 **Aggregation Relationship**

Identifying Aggregation

Identify aggregation by looking for assembly and part objects. For example, a car is an assembly with a motor part. Look for objects that cannot exist without other objects. For example, an invoice cannot exist without a product line item. Look for objects that are so closely associated that they are destroyed if the first object is destroyed. For example, if an invoice is destroyed then the product line items are destroyed.

Aggregation Class Diagram

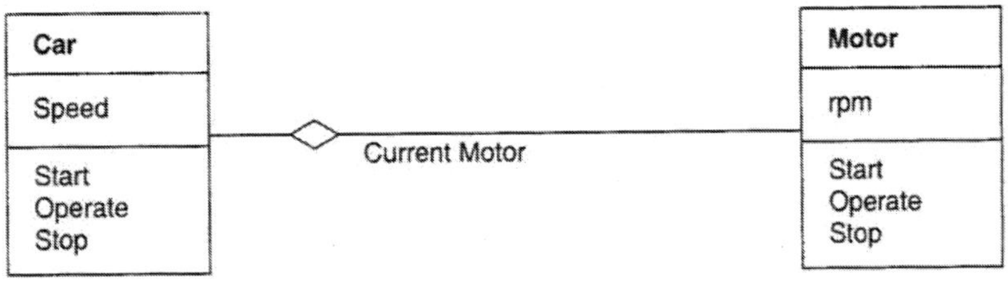

1.6.3 Generalization or Specialization or Inheritance

A generalization or specialization relationship indicates a commonality between a super class and subclasses also known as inheritance. It indicates that the super class and subclass have common attributes, operations, and relationships. It indicates an "is a" or "type of" relationship. For example, a vehicle super class may define common attributes, operations, and relationships for a car subclass. A car "is a" vehicle. In a family inheritance grandfather super class will be parent for father and father class become parent for child class. The generalization specialization relationship is implemented in programming languages with inheritance. The generalization specialization symbol is a triangle on a solid line.

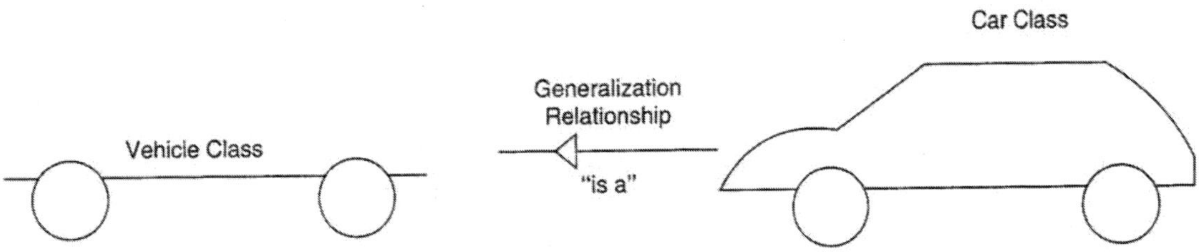

FIGURE 1.6 **Generalization Specialization**

The generalization specialization relationship is implemented in object-oriented programming languages like C++ or Java in form of inheritance. **Inheritance** is the implementation mechanism for the generalization specialization relationship. In **single inheritance** a subclass has only one superclass. In **multiple inheritance** a subclass has two or more superclasses. Inheritance is the mechanism used in object-oriented programming languages to permit a subclass to share attributes and operations defined in the superclasses. For example the subclass MCA2 semester can share the attributes and operations from the superclass MCA. The subclass MCA2 may add attributes and operations as its own. The subclass MCA2 may redefine attributes and operations.

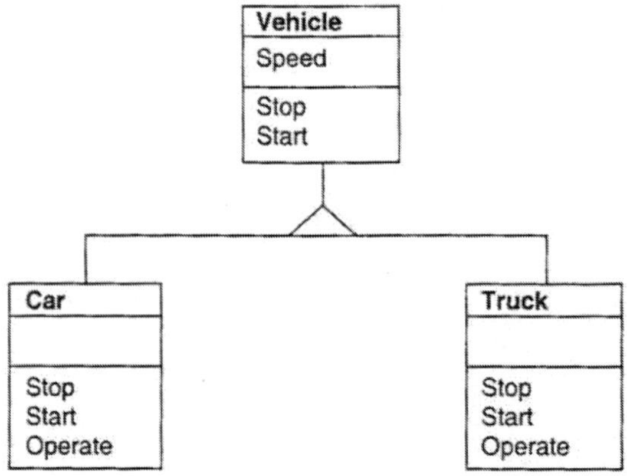

The diagram in the figure above shows the Vehicle superclass and the Car and Truck subclasses. The superclass attribute speed is inherited by the subclasses.

Generalization Specialization to Develop Quality Software

How effectively you model generalization specialization in class diagram affect the quality of the software in terms of correctness, reliability, extendibility, and reusability. For example, the use of generalization specialization leads to specialized classes that can be easily modified or changed out without affecting other classes. This improves the extendibility of the software.

The use of generalization specialization with polymorphic operations is a software quality technique. It supports the creation of understandable, extendible software. Always identify a superclass with general operations. Then identify subclasses with the same named operations (polymorphic operations). Now create a specific implementation of each polymorphic operation in the subclasses. Each subclass has the responsibility to provide the correct, specific actions for the polymorphic operation. Later, when we want to expand the system we add a new subclass with new implementations of the polymorphic operations. We can add a new subclass with new implementations of the polymorphic operations relatively easily without adversely affecting other classes in the system.

1.6.4 Interaction

An interaction relationship is used to setup call, message passing or communication between objects. An interaction relationship may be described as "calls", "interacts", "messages " or "communicates" among objects. For example, the object car1 can "calls" the object motor1.

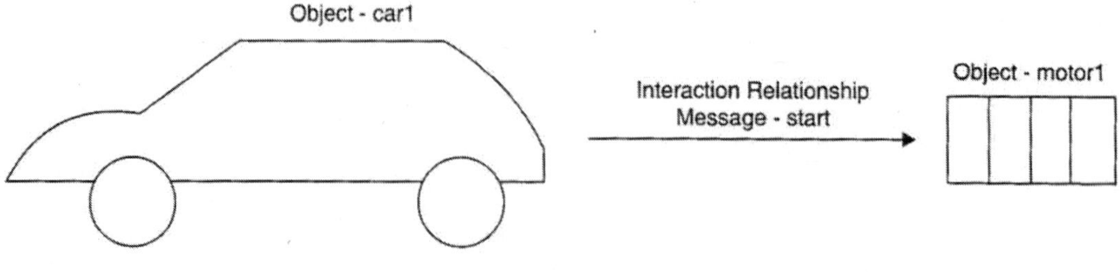

FIGURE 1.7 **Interaction**

Interaction involves stimulus response behavior with an event or message. An **event** is an occurrence at a point in time that is a stimulus for a system or an object. The term event is very general and refers to any stimulus for a system or an object. There are several forms of events representing an interaction relationship:

- A **system event** is a stimulus for a system. An **input event** is an incoming stimulus for the system being modeled. An **output event** is an outgoing stimulus from the system being modeled to an interacting system. Input and output events are shown on a system interaction diagram as arrows.
- An **event for a state-based object** is a stimulus that may result in transition to a new state. An event for a state-based object is shown on a state diagram as an arrow.
- A **message** is a stimulus from one object to another object. A message invokes an operation. The full specification of a message consists of the receiver object name, the operation name, the input parameters, and the output (return) parameters. In object oriented some methodologies, messages may be shown on a class diagram since messages are defined within a class. However, messages are executed between objects. The message symbol is a solid arrow pointing in the direction of the receiver.

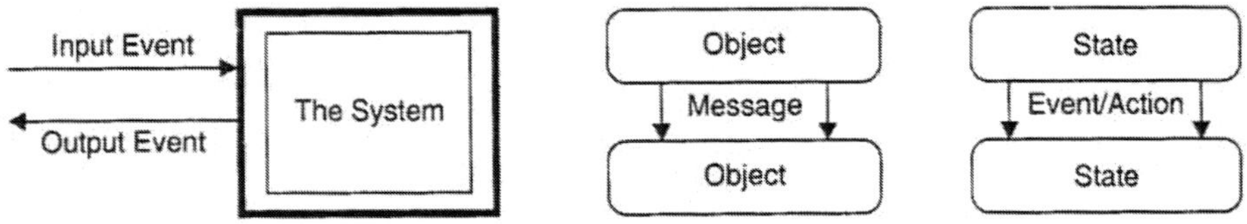

FIGURE 1.8 **Several Forms of Events**

1.7 OBJECT MODELING

The three main types in Object Oriented modeling are:

1. Object model
2. Dynamic model
3. Functional model

These three models are used to setup a logical framework to model or design systems and classes. They given us opportunity to examine a problem from different points of view. They help us to design and develop quality software that will be correct, reliable, and modifiable in future.

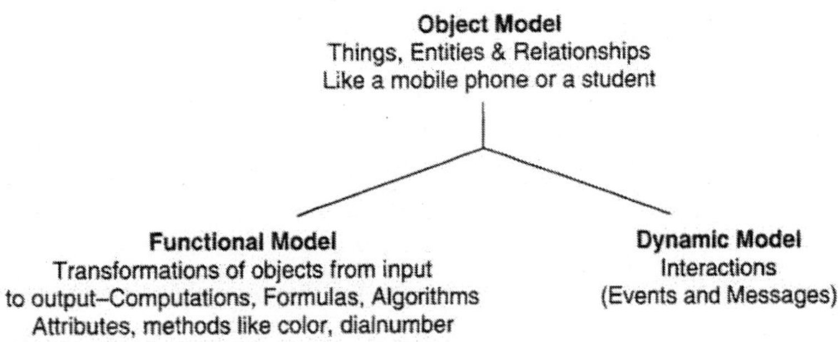

FIGURE 1.9 **Three Types of Modeling**

All Object-Oriented methodologies use these three models in some form with different diagrams and text specifications. If you have designed correct model you can convert it in a computer software form using any object oriented language like C++ or Java.

1.8 SAMPLE OBJECT MODEL

In a sample object model we will use example of a mobile handset system and a coffee machine. As we have discussed that there are three types of model or points of view in Object-oriented Modeling. First we look at a problem from the object point of view (Object Model). Start with static structure of the entities you are taking as a problem. It is just like think about the basic picture of the entity like a mobile handset, your own Nokia or Motorola. This will give you the static structure of the handset like body, color, buttons, screen etc. In modeling terms you will think about the static structure of system, classes, and relationships. After that look at your object your mobile phone as a dynamic point of view (Dynamic Model). We are interested now to stimulus response behavior of objects in a problem over time. It is like taking working position of an entity like coffee machine. This working position will give you some operations like switch on the mobile, dial a number, send a SMS, and go to mailbox etc. In modeling terms you think about the stimulus response behavior of the handset over time. You can say the phone is responding to the user events (stimuli) like "send message", "start internet", and "go to sound clips" with the appropriate responses. Now in next part look at the problem from a functional point of view. We are interested in what is transformed or changed in the problem. It is like looking your coffee machine. Something go into the machine (water, sugar, coffee powder etc) and there is a transformation of the inputs into outputs your one cup of hot coffee. In modeling terms we see the transformations of inputs to outputs in operations.

In Object-oriented modeling you have to design system level and class level points of view. Initially you will describe a system from an external point of view to determine overall system requirements, boundary, interfaces, and behavior. Then describe the system from an internal point of view your class view to describe classes, objects, and relationships within the system. This is describing a system with different levels of abstractions or to design abstract classes for your system. The highest level of abstraction is the system view which is very general. The lower level of abstraction is the class view which is more detailed. For example, in a Car system design you will model the Car Simulation System on paper first, then model the Car as a class in the Car Simulation System.

Currency Control System

A sample Currency Control System is a Software program that interacts with currency control equipment to store and exchange various international currencies. A user can exchange currency in various forms using this system. A currency exchange rate can be a float that is used to convert an amount of an input currency to compute the amount of an output currency, like the currency exchange rate of a US dollar to a Deutschemark is can set to 1.5. There is an input amount that a user inputs and an output amount that a user receives during an exchange.

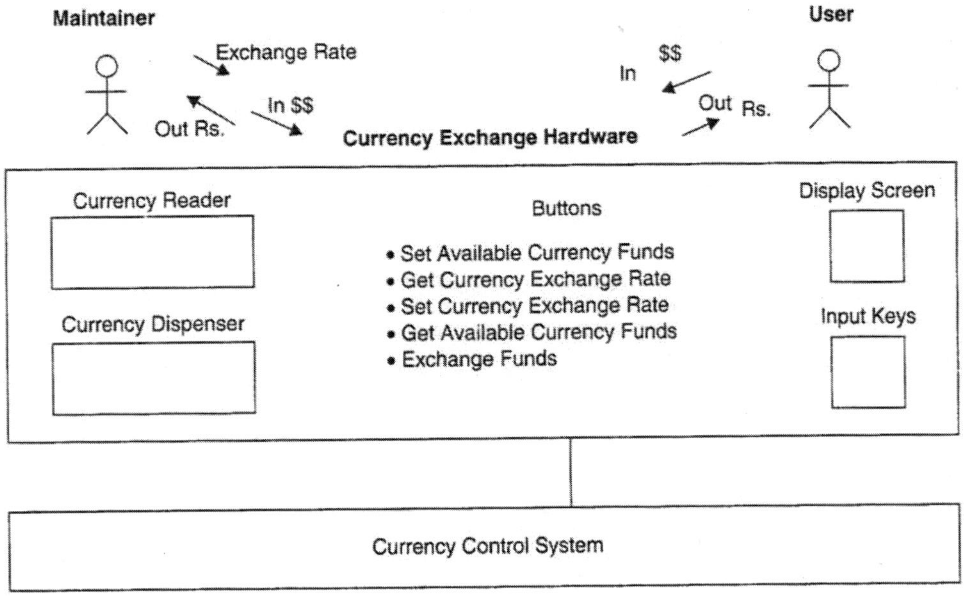

1.8.1 System View

To design a system view there is a need to create diagrams and text specifications for the system as a whole without thinking about the inside part of the system. We always start with an external point of view. You can think some questions also like:

- What is the proposed system?
- What is the system boundary or limitation (What it can do, what can not)?
- What is the system behavior?
- What types of events will be there to respond by system?
- What are the inputs and outputs (objects) that are used by the system?

In the system view we use the object, dynamic, and functional points of view. From the object view, we identify the key entities that the system interfaces will use like in Amrapali Institute system students, faculty, library, classes etc will be the entities. We identify other systems that are associated with the system. From the dynamic view, we identify the time based behavior of the system. We identify input events, output events, and states for the system. From the functional view, we identify input objects, output objects, and system operations.

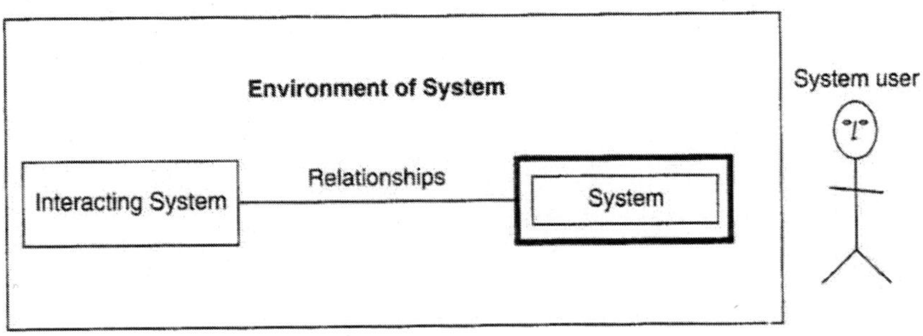

FIGURE 1.10 **Modeling the System in the System Environment**

1.8.2 Class View

After modeling of system view next is to design the class view, again there is a need to design or write diagrams and text specifications for classes and relationships in the system. That can be think as an internal point of view. Key questions can be at this points:

- What and how many the classes will be in the proposed system?
- What will be the relationships between the classes like faculty and students class in the proposed system?
- What will be the interactions between objects in the proposed system?
- What will be the states of objects in the proposed system?
- What are the transformations of objects performed by class and object operations like in coffee machine example?

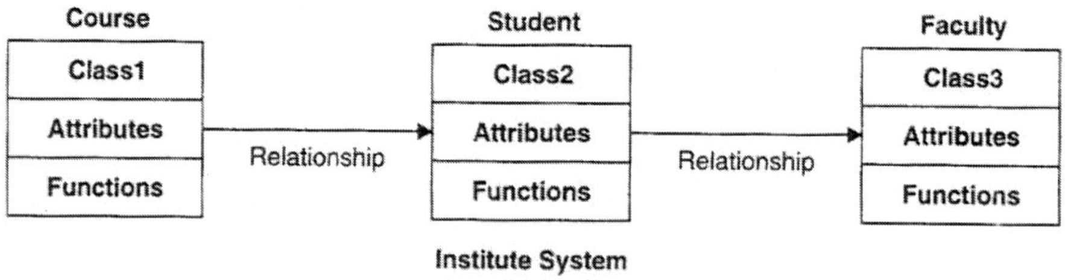

FIGURE 1.11 **Modeling of Classes and Relationships in the System**

1.9 ABSTRACT CLASSES

In object-oriented programming, **classes** are used to group related variables and functions. A class describes a collection of encapsulated instance variables and methods (functions), possibly with implementation of those types together with a constructor function that can be used to create objects of the class.

An **abstract class,** or *abstract base class* (ABC), is one that is designed *only* as a parent class and from which child classes may be derived, and which is not itself suitable for instantiation. Abstract classes are often used to represent abstract concepts or entities. The incomplete features of the abstract class are then shared by a group of sibling sub-classes which add different variations of the missing pieces. In C++, an abstract class is defined as a class having at least one pure virtual method, *i.e.*, an abstract method, which may or may not possess an implementation.

Abstract classes are superclasses which contain abstract methods and are defined such that concrete subclasses are to extend them by implementing the methods. The behaviors defined by such a class are *"generic"* and much of the class will be undefined and unimplemented. Before a class derived from an abstract class can be instantiated, it must implement particular methods for all the abstract methods of its parent classes.

In computing, when specifying an **abstract class**, the programmer is referring to a **class** which has elements that are meant to be implemented by inheritance. The abstraction of the class methods to be implemented by the sub-classes is meant to simplify software development.

1.10 MULTIPLE INHERITANCE

In object-oriented programming (OOP), **inheritance** describes a relationship between two types, or classes, of objects in which one is said to be a "subclass" or "child" of the other. The child inherits features of the parent, allowing for shared functionality. For example, one might create a variable class "Mammal" with features such as eating, reproducing, etc.; then define a subtype "Dog" that inherits those features without having to explicitly program them, while adding new features like "barking".

Sometimes a single class can inherit feature of multiple classes like your mobile phone having features of phone, song player, intenet browser, calculator etc. This is known as Multiple inheritance. **Multiple inheritance** refers to a feature of object-oriented programming languages in which a class can inherit behaviors and features from more than one superclass. This contrasts with **single inheritance**, where a class inherits from only one superclass.

Inheritance is also sometimes called **generalization**, because the **is-a** relationships represent a hierarchy between classes of objects. For instance, a "fruit" is a generalization of "apple", "orange", "mango" and many others. One can consider fruit to be an abstraction of apple, orange, etc. Conversely, since apples are fruit (an apple **is-a** fruit), apples may naturally inherit all the properties common to all fruit.

An advantage of inheritance is that modules with sufficiently similar interfaces can share a lot of code, reducing the complexity of the program. You can reuse the classes, functions and codes in a sotware, that reduce the cost of your software.

1.10.1 Specialization

One common reason to use inheritance is to create specializations of existing classes or objects. This is often called *subtyping* when applied to classes. In specialization, the new class or object has data or behavior aspects that are not part of the inherited class. For example, a "Bank Account" class might have data for an "account number", "owner", and "balance". An "Interest Bearing Account" class might inherit "Bank Account" and then add data for "interest rate" and "interest accrued" alongwith behavior for calculating interest earned. That means a child class can inhert features of parent class with having its own new features.

1.11 METADATA

Metadata (Greek *meta* "after" and Latin *data* "information") are data that describe other data. Generally, a set of metadata describes a single object or set of data, called a resource. Example: 243639 is data, and with no additional context is meaningless. With the additional "metadata" of giving 243639 a meaningful name of "Pin Code" assuming Pin Code is a part of a postal address, you can then understand that 243639 represents Haldwani.

1.11.1 Difference between Data and Metadata

Usually it is not possible to distinguish between (raw) data and metadata because of the following effects:

- Data can be both raw data and metadata at the same time. The headline of a text is both part of the text, *i.e.*, data, and title of the text, *i.e.*, metadata.

- Data and metadata can change their roles. A poem, as such, would be regarded data, but if there were a song that used it as lyrics, the whole poem could be attached to an audio file as metadata. Thus, the interpretation depends on the point of view.
- It is possible to create meta-meta-...-metadata. As, according to the common definition, metadata themselves are data, it is possible to create metadata about metadata, metadata about metadata about metadata and so on. Though at first look this sounds useless, it can be essential to archive metadata about metadata, *e.g.*, to keep track of where the metadata came from when merging two documents.

1.11.2 Applications

Metadata have become important on the World Wide Web because of the need to find useful information from the mass of information available. Manually-created metadata add value because they ensure consistency. If one webpage about a topic contains a word or phrase, then all webpages about that topic should contain that same word or phrase. They also ensure variety, so that if one topic has two names, each of these names will be used. For example, an article about *Sport Utility Vehicles* would also be given the metadata keywords '4 wheel drives', '4WDs' and 'four wheel drives', as this is how they are known in some countries.

Examples of metadata for an audio CD include the MusicBrainz project, MP3 files have metadata tags in a format called ID3.

Metadata are more properly called an ontology or schema when structured into a hierarchical arrangement. Both terms describe "what exists" for some purpose or to enable some action. For instance, the arrangement of subject headings in a library catalog serves not only as a guide to finding books on a particular subject in the stacks, but also as a guide to what subjects "exist" in the library's own ontology and how more specialized topics are related to or derived from the more general subject headings.

Metadata are frequently stored in a central location and used to help organizations standardize their data. This information is typically stored in a Metadata Registry.

1.12 CANDIDATE KEY

In the relational *database* model a **candidate key** of a relation variable say x is a set of attributes of that x such that:

1. At all times it holds in the relation assigned to that variable that there are no two distinct tuples with the same values for these attributes
2. There is not a proper subset for which (1) holds. Since a superkey is defined as a set of attributes for which (1) holds we can also define candidate keys as minimal superkeys, *i.e.*, superkeys of which no proper subset is also a superkey.

The importance of candidate keys is that they tell us how we can identify individual tuples in a relation. As such they are one of the most important types of database constraint that should be specified when designing a database schema. Since a relation is a set, it holds that every relation will have at least one candidate key (because the entire heading is always a superkey). Since in some RDBMSs tables may also represent multisets (which strictly means these DBMSs are not relational), it is an important design rule to specify explicitly at least one candidate key for each relation. For practical reasons RDBMSs usually require that for each relation one of its candidate keys is declared as the primary key, which means that it is considered as the preferred way to identify individual tuples. Foreign keys, for example, are usually required to reference such a primary key and not any of the other candidate keys.

In other words, a candidate key is a field or combination of fields that can act as a primary key field for that table to uniquely identify each record in that table. For example a relation *Employee(Name, Address, Dept)* probably represents employees and these are likely to be uniquely identified by a combination of *Name* and *Address* which is therefore a superkey, and unless the same holds for only *Name* or only *Address*, then this combination is also a candidate key.

1.13 CONSTRAINTS

An object-constraint is a constraint on the properties of an object. Such objects can represent arbitrary systems of objects and parameters; this theory puts no restriction on the nature of the object (*e.g.*, it might be a component, or syntatic structure, or a list of parameters). The purpose for distinguishing object constraints from parametric constraints is to allow for a modular scope of a constraint.

Formally, an object-constraint is a constraint whose constraint expression is a sentence with one free variable. That variable is not universally quantified; instead, it stands for the object being constrained. The semantics of the constraint expressions is given by the predicate SATISFIES-CONSTRAINT, which associates the variable with some specific object.

1.14 DIFFERENT OBJECT-ORIENTED METHODOLOGIES

An object-oriented methodology has a defined set of entities like system, class, object, graphic symbols, diagrams, forms, rules, and procedures. It is a process that generally covers the entire software lifecycle from requirements to implementation phase to develop a quality software. Many CASE tool supports a subset graphic notation for several object-oriented methodologies, Like:

- Rumbaugh Object Modeling Technique (OMT)
- Coad/Yourdon Object-Oriented Analysis and Design (OOA/OOD)
- Booch Object-Oriented Design (OOD)
- Shlaer Mellor OOA/OOD

1.14.1 Rumbaugh Object Modeling Technique (OMT)

This Object-Oriented methodology is documented in *Object-Oriented Modeling and Design* by James Rumbaugh. It has a strong data modeling origin. It has a very comprehensive graphic notation. Analysis in OMT consists of the Object Model, Dynamic Model, and Functional Model which has been discussed earlier. Analysis is followed by system design and detailed design are main part of OMT.

1.14.2 Coad/Yourdon Object-Oriented Analysis and Design (OOA/OOD)

This Object Oriented methodology is documented in *Object-Oriented Analysis* and *Object-Oriented Design* by Peter Coad and Ed Yourdon [Coad-91a and Coad-91b]. It has a strong data modeling origin. It has a simple graphic notation. OOA consists of identifying and organizing classes from different points of view called layers. OOD consists of refining the OOA model for the human interface, problem domain, data management, and concurrent task management.

1.14.3 Booch Object-Oriented Design (OOD)

This Object-Oriented methodology is documented in *Object-Oriented Design with Applications* by Grady Booch [Booch-94]. It has a very strong real-time and message passing origin. It has an extensive, comprehensive graphic notation. OOD consists of modeling a system by identifying, organizing, and specifying subsystems, classes, objects, implementation modules and processes.

1.14.4 Shlaer Mellor OOA/OOD

This Object-Oriented methodology is documented in *Object Lifecycles - Modeling the World in States* by Sally Shlaer and Stephen Mellor [Shlaer-92]. OOA consists of information (data) models, state models, and process models similar to the OMT object model, dynamic model, and functional model. OOD consists of refining the OOA models for an implementation environment.

REVIEW QUESTIONS

1. Differentiate between generalization, association and aggregation. **(UTU-2001-02, 2003)**
2. What is an abstract class? Give suitable example from real life. **(UTU-2001-02)**
3. Design and draw class structure for a house structure, Make realistic assumption about room, kitchen etc. **(UTU-2001-02)**
4. What is Metadata. **(UTU-2001-02)**
5. Represent association using diagram between following classes: **(UTU-2001-02)**

1. Employee	Company
2. Capital	Country
3. Computer	User
4. Car	Wheel

6. Describe Object model, functional model and dynamic model. **(UTU-2001-02,2003,2004,2005)**
7. Draw an object model of a workstation window management system like Xwindow. **(UTU-2003)**
8. Draw a class diagram that shows multiple inheritance from overlapping classes. **(UTU-2003)**
9. Explain instances with suitable examples. **(UTU-2003)**
10. Design an object diagram for a library book checkout system that shows the date a book is due and the late charges for an overdue book as derived objects. **(UTU-2004)**
11. Prepare a state diagram for making a transaction in an ATM machine. **(UTU-2004)**
12. How does inheritance is differ from generalization? Explain with example. **(UTU-2005)**
13. What is aggregation? Explain with suitable example and diagram. **(UTU-2005)**
14. What is object modeling technique? Draw OMT Object model for participants registration system in a seminar. **(UTU-2005)**
15. Apply booch's methodology for object-oriented analysis and design specification of sales office automation. **(UTU-2005)**

Chapter 2

DYNAMIC MODELING

2.1 DYNAMIC MODEL

In the object model, You will describe the system in for of classes and relationships. This object model will give you the static structure of a system. In the dynamic model now you have to the stimulus response behavior of a system that means when you will input your commands or actions what will be the response of the system in form of output like when you will press dial button of your phone it will dial the given number. You think about dynamic, time oriented view of the system.

2.2 STATE DIAGRAM IN DYNAMIC MODEL

Using state diagram you can show complex stimulus response behavior for a system or objects of a class. Stare diagram is a directed graph whose nodes represent states and directed arcs shows transitions. The directed arc shows the event that triggers the transition with the applicable condition and actions. The purpose of the state diagram is to specify stimulus response logic for a system or class of objects. It specifies the pattern of states, events, conditions, and actions.

State

A **state** represents a mode of control that has a unique combination of events, conditions, actions, and next state. A state is static form which wait for an event to occur. While in a state, a defined set of rules, laws, and policies apply. A state is like a manager or coordinator that knows how to respond to each event according to his rules, laws, and procedures. There is an **initial state** that is entered when the object is created. There is a **termination state** that is entered prior to the object being destroyed. The states for a Mobile set can be "Off" and "Operating". States may be shown in a generalization specialization hierarchy in which generalization states (super classes) define the most general, common behavior and specialization states (subclasses) define specialized behavior for an object in the specialization state.

Event

An **event** is an occurrence at a point in time that is a stimulus for a system or an object. The events for a car can be "start ", "operate ", and "stop". An event may be represented as an event object, such as "The_Start_Event" or as a message signifying that the event has occurred such as "open()". As an object identity the attributes of the event object. As a message identify any parameters that are passed in the event message. An event may be a system event that is passed to the system being modeled, such as "start". Alternatively an event may be an internal event that is sent from an object in the system, such as "permission denied ".

Input Event

An **input event** is something that occurs at a point in time that is a stimulus for a system or an object of the system. An event has no time duration. An event is an occurrence that a system or an object must respond to. Forms of events include user events, physical events, and time events. A user event is initiated by an interacting system such as "user pressed a button" or "user selected a menu item ". A physical event occurs in the physical word such as "temperature increased above a point". A time event is a time occurrence such as "time is 2 o'clock" or "request time-out ".

Output Event

An **output event** is something that occurs as a result of an input event. An output event is frequently an event that is a stimulus to an interacting system. An output event may have information attached to it such as "time of event". An output event can be implemented as an object such as "CarStarted output event" or as a message such as "RecordCarStarted ()". It is an occurrence that a system initiates or causes to happen.

Operation

An **action** is an operation such as dialnumber() in response to an event. Actions include updating an attribute, sending a message, creating or destroying an object, or similar action. The actions for a mobile object can be "Mobile.dialnumber()", "Mobile.sendsms()", or "Mobile.searchphonebook()". An action may be instantaneous such as "Mobile.off()" or may be continuous activity, such as "call by mobile". A continuous activity is indicated on a state diagram with "do:", such as "do:mobilecall". An action may lead to a system output event that is passed from the system, such as "car started". Alternatively an action may be an internal response to an internal event, such as "wrong number status".

Methods

Practical implementations of operations of a system in any programming language like C++ or Java are known as methods. An Object of class can call the method like form1.show(). In previous example show() is a method and form1 is a object of window class.

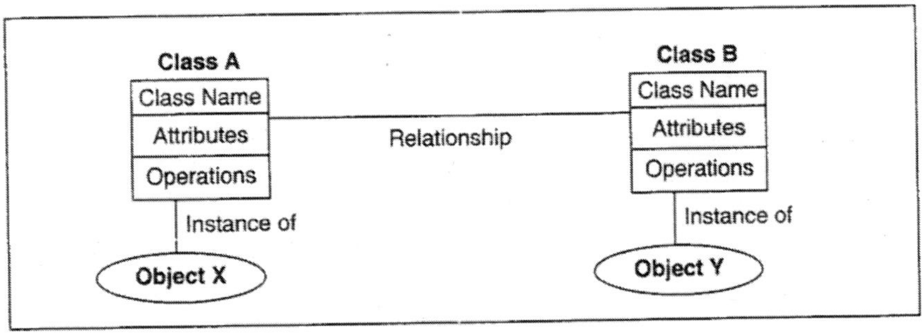

FIGURE 2.1 **Parts of a System**

Condition

A **condition** is a logical value (true or false) that is valid over a period of time that affects transitions from one state to another. A **condition** is a Boolean expression signifying TRUE or FALSE that you can write using an IF Condition like If x=TRUE THEN DoSomeTHING. Examples of conditions can be like one mobile number is in your network range or not.

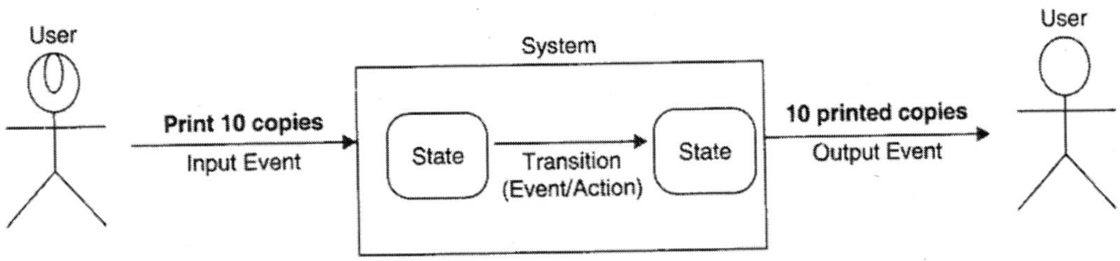

Parts of dynamic modeling (State, Events, Method)

FIGURE 2.2 **State diagram**

2.3 SYSTEM USE CASES

A use case is a specific way of using a system. The system use case describe the major functions of the system from a user's point of view. There are four key entities in use cases: actor, use case, interaction, and system.

Actor

An **actor** is an outside entity that interacts with the system. Actors include human users, machines, devices, and other systems. Typical actors are customer, user, manager, supervisor, printer, network communications device, etc. An actor is a user type or category. An actor defines a role that a user can play, like customer versus operator. Actors interact and communicate with the system. Frequently, an actor interacts with the system through an interacting system. For example, a customer interacts with a bank ATM system with ATM User Interface System. Sometimes, an actor is an interacting system, like a printer is an actor as well as interacting system.

Use Case

A **use case** is a specific way of using a system by using some part of its functionality, like "printapage". Each use case is a complete sequence of interactions input and output events. An

input event is something that occurs at a point in time that is a stimulus for a system. An **output event** is something that occurs at a point in time that is sent from the system. A complete scenario is an input event leading to an output event. Typically, an actor initiates an input event that leads to an output event. For example, the actor "User" initiates the input event "printapage". The event is detected by the system. The system issues a series of output events to the printer. A use case may have sub-use cases which reflect a portion or specialized functionality of a system.

Interacting System

An **interacting system** like an actor in use case can be a human user or other entity that initiates an input event, indicates that an input event has occurred, receives a output event say response, or interacts with the system in any way. An interacting system is external or outside the system. An interacting system can be a human users, hardware devices, software programs. The key point about an interacting system is that it is external to the system and that it interacts with the system with input and output events. The following are some sample software systems and interacting systems: Window media player buttons controls, DVD player control Device, Volume Device, Automatic Teller Machine User Interface Devices in windows, Bank Interface Devices etc.

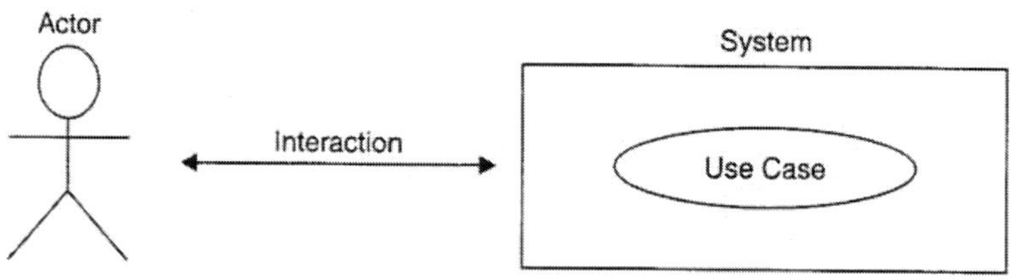

FIGURE 2.3 **Use case diagram**

2.4 NESTED STATE DIAGRAM

In dynamic model a simple state diagram is used to show only top level or external level dependency among actions, if you want to show low level activities actions of system then you have to use nested state diagram. In nested state diagram you can expend it upto lowest level and each lower level state will represent one step of the activity. With the help of nested state diagram you can show internal or sub and sub-sub actions of your system.

2.5 CONCURRENCY

Concurrency within the state of an object arises when you think that object can be divided into subsets of attributes or links, each of which will have a new state sub diagram. The state of the object comprise one state from each sub diagram. The sub diagram need not to be independent unit because a same event can cause transition in more than one sub diagram. Concurrency within a single composite state of an object is shown by partitioning the composite state in sub diagrams with dotted lines.

Aggregation Concurrency

A Dynamic model describes a set of concurrent objects which have their own states and state diagrams. The objects in a system are inherently concurrent and can change state independently.

The state of the entire system cannot be represented by a single state in a single object, it has to be the product of states of all the objects. A state diagram for a system is a collection of all state diagrams of each components. Aggregation implies concurrency. The aggregation state is equal to the combined state of all the component diagrams.

Aggregation is known as and relationship. If you take example of a Car system, it can be a aggregation of many components and their states.

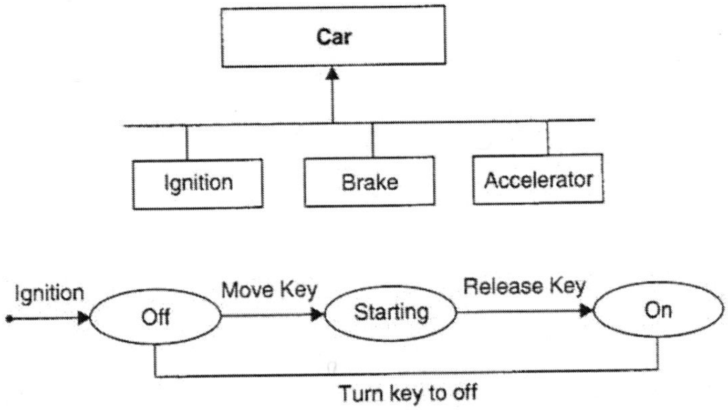

FIGURE 2.4 **Aggregation concurrency**

2.6 RELATION OF OBJECT AND DYNAMIC MODEL

The **object model** provides a static or structural point of view to describe the system, classes, and relationships. You will define the attributes and functions / operations of your system in that while the **dynamic model** provides a stimulus response time based point of view to describe events, messages, and different states of your system.

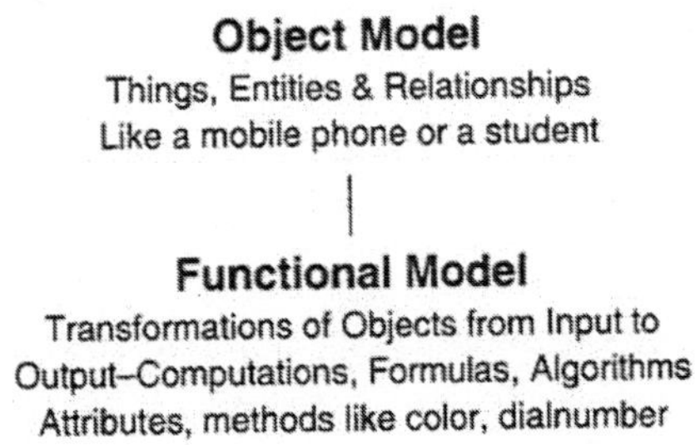

FIGURE 2.5 **Relation of object and dynamic model**

2.7 ADVANCE CONCEPTS

The modern dynamic model is used to express and model the behavior of the system over time. It includes support for activity diagrams, state diagrams, sequence diagrams and extensions including *business process modeling.*

Sequence Diagrams

Sequence diagrams are used to display the interaction between users, screens, objects and entities within the system. It provides a sequential map of message passing between objects over time. Frequently these diagrams are placed under Use Cases in the model to illustrate the use case scenario - how a user will interact with the system and what happens internally to get the work done. Often, the objects are represented using special stereotyped icons, as in the example below. The object labelled Login Screen is shown using the User Interface icon. The object labelled SecurityManager is shown using the Controller icon. The Object labelled users is shown using the Entity icon.

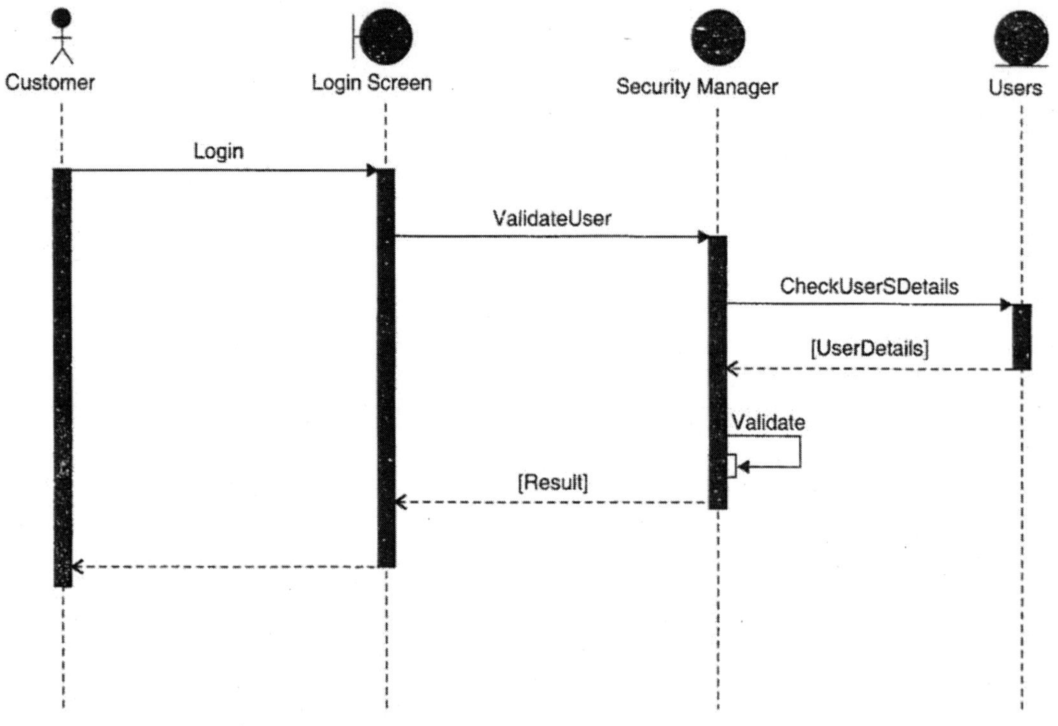

FIGURE 2.6 **Sequence diagram**

Activity Diagrams

Activity diagrams are used to show how different workflows in the system are constructed, how they start and the possibly many decision paths that can be taken from start to finish. They may also illustrate the where parallel processing may occur in the execution of some activities.

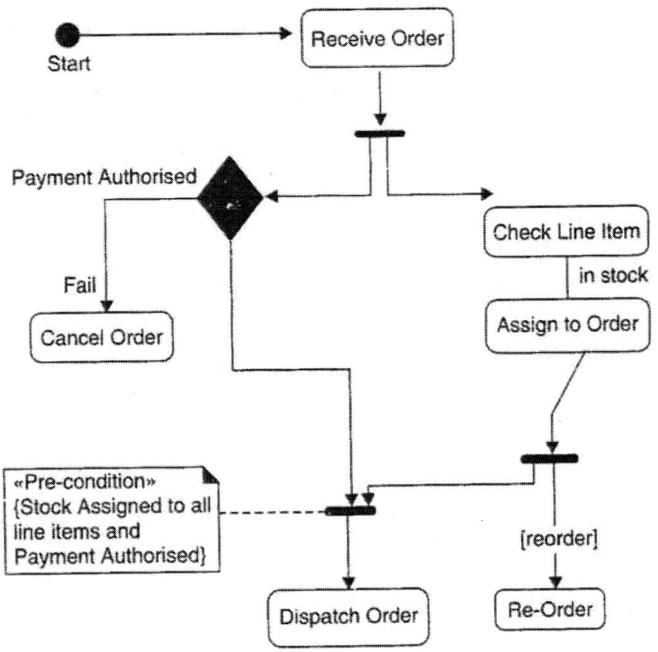

FIGURE 2.7 **Activity Diagram**

State Charts

State charts are used to detail the transitions or changes of state an object can go through in the system. They show how an object moves from one state to another and the rules that govern that change. State charts typically have a start and end condition.

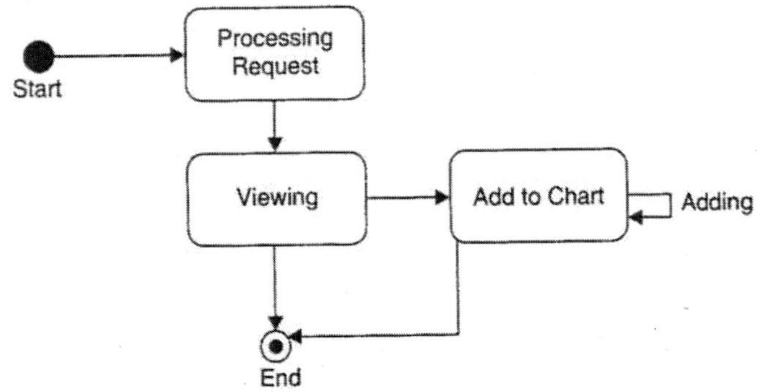

FIGURE 2.8 **State charts**

2.8 SAMPLE DYNAMIC MODEL

In chapter 1, we have used a sample model of currency control or exchange machine as Object Model, now we will design dynamic model of that machine. To design Dynamic model we have to think about events, states, operations and conditions of the machine.

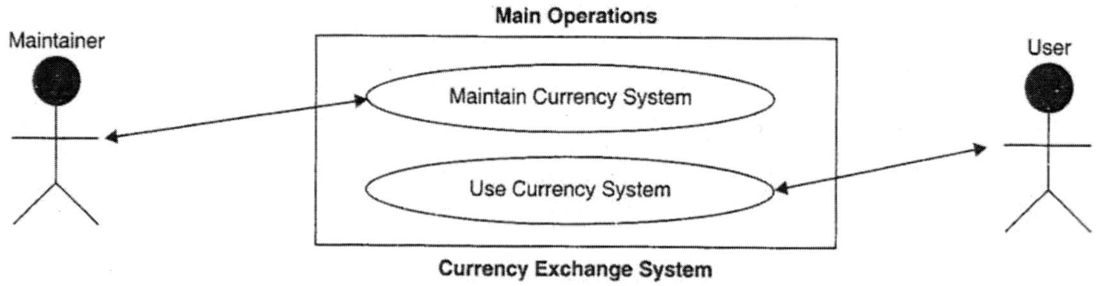

Coffee Control System

A Coffee Control System is a Software program attached with any Coffee Equipment to control coffee item information. The Coffee Control System should responds to some commands that can be initiated by a user or supervisor to fill and dispense items like coffee, cups, sugar, and cream and functions like Fill_Cup, Fill_Coffee, Fill_Sugar, Fill_Cream, Get_Current_Cups etc.

The Coffee Control System will responds to these commands by returning information and by issuing the following responses to the Coffee Equipment: Show_Status, Fill_Cup, Fill_Coffee, Fill_Sugar, Fill_Cream etc.

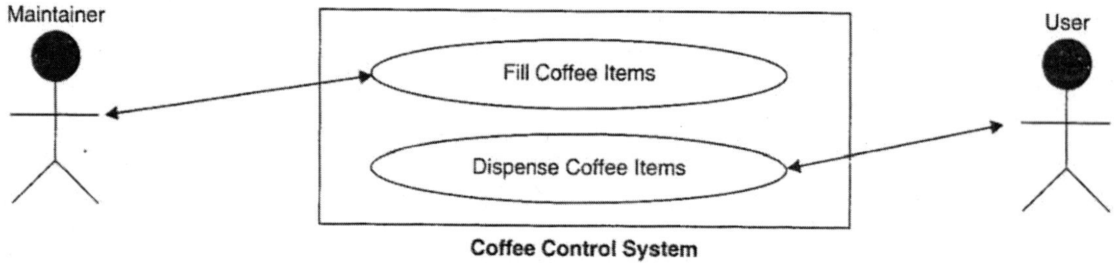

REVIEW QUESTIONS

1. What is Dynamic model? What is the difference between dynamic and object model? **(UTU-2002,2004,05)**
2. Identify various states in which a floppy drive in a computer system can exist. Draw state transition diagram. **(UTU-2002)**
3. How is concurrency within state of a single object represented? **(UTU-2002)**
4. Discuss aggregation concurrency and concurrency within objects with the help of suitable state diagrams. **(UTU-2003,05)**
5. Prepare a state diagram for making a transition in an ATM machine. **(UTU-2004)**
6. Prepare state diagram for twin tub semi automatic washing machine having usual controls in that. **(UTU-2004)**
7. What are nested state diagrams? Why are they useful? Explain with suitable example. **(UTU-2004)**
8. Explain the relationship between object and dynamic model. Include an example also. **(UTU-2005)**
9. What is the role of state diagram in dynamic model ling? **(UTU-2005)**
10. Draw state diagram for your mobile phone.

Chapter 3 FUNCTIONAL MODELING

3.1 FUNCTIONAL MODEL

When you start object oriented system design and modeling you start with a static structure of a system and classes in the system object model. In next phase you need to identify system operations and object operations. You have used the dynamic stimulus response behavior of the system and objects in the system in the system dynamic model in which operations are invoked in earlier chapters. Now you must look at each operation and define the transformation of inputs to outputs in the system functional model. In functional model you will define the transformation of system and its parts in terms of computation, algorithms, and formulas. The functional model describes transformations of object values in operations from an input point of view to an output point of view.

3.2 MODELING OPERATIONS IN THE FUNCTIONAL MODEL

Once you have designed or specified the system models, the object model and the dynamic model, you should specify all operations in the functional model. The functional model is the set of transformations and correctness assertions, like pre conditions, post conditions, and invariants. A transformation is a description of how an object value like percentage of a student object may be correctly changed in a formula, expression, table, etc. An assertion is a rule or expression for correctness, like totalmarks must always be greater than zero. An operation precondition is a rule or expression that must be satisfied before the execution of an operation for correct results like one must have amount in account before withdraw from ATM machine. An operation postcondition is a rule or expression that is satisfied upon the correct execution of an operation like update the closingbalance after successful with draw of amount. An invariant is a general rule or expression that must be satisfied at all times by all applicable operations. An exception is an abnormal execution error condition, ATMcashempty Error or nolinkError that may be raised to signal that an operation cannot be executed correctly. In the car example, the start operation has a precondition and postcondition. The precondition for the start operation is that the petrol must be greater than zero. The postcondition of the start operation is the verification that the correct value of petrolQuantity has been computed. In the functional model, you update class specifications with transformations and correctness assertions.

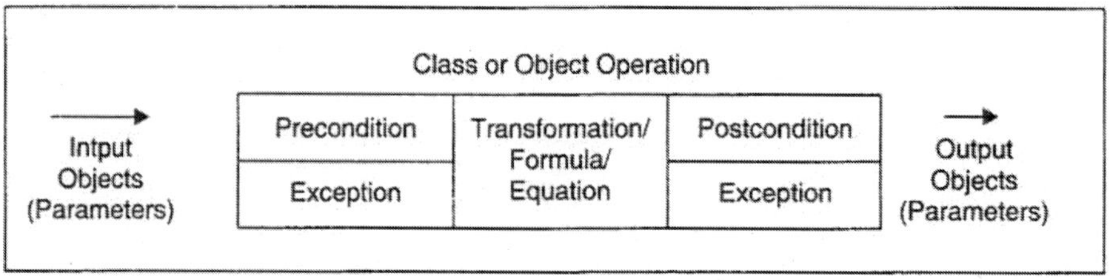

FIGURE 3.1 **Functional modeling**

The functional model is important for many reasons. First, transformations (operations) are important because they accomplish work required by the system requirements. Second, identifying transformations (operations) leads to identifying the system input objects, system output objects, and system operations. Third, identifying operation preconditions, postconditions, and exceptions help create highly reliable operations. Fourth, operations are implemented by coding the transformation equations, preconditions, postconditions, and exceptions.

3.3 SPECIFYING OPERATIONS

In functional modeling a transformation may occur in the following forms of operations:

System Operation is an operation for the system as a whole. A system operation receives an input object and changes an output object. A system operation may access or modify a system attribute. A sample system operation for a bank ATM system can be "Cashwithdraw".

Class Operation is an operation defined in a class that accesses or modifies a class attribute value. A class operation affects all objects of the class. When a class operation is invoked to change a class attribute value, all objects of the class share this attribute value.

Object Operation is an operation defined in a class that accesses or modifies an attribute value. An operation may receive an input parameter and may send an output parameter. A sample operation in a bank ATM Account class is "updateAccountBalance". This operation modifies the attribute "custaccountBalance".

3.4 DATA FLOW DIAGRAMS

Graphical description of a system's data and how the processes transform the data is known as Data Flow Diagram (or DFD). Unlike detail flowcharts, Data Flow Diagrams do not supply detailed descriptions of modules but graphically describe a system's data and how the data interact with the system. To construct data flow diagrams, you will use:

- Arrows
- Circles / ellipse

- Open-ended boxes
- Squares

An arrow identifies data flow - data in motion. It is a pipeline through which information flows. Like the rectangle in flowcharts, circles stand for a process that converts data/into information. An open-ended box represents a data store or data at rest, or a temporary repository of data. A square defines a source (originator) or destination of system data.

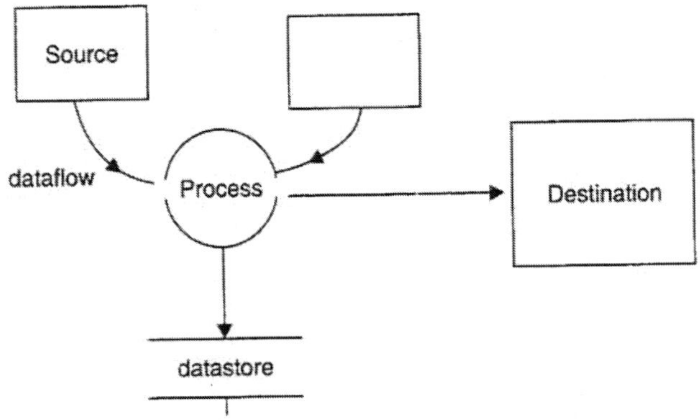

FIGURE 3.2 **Data flow diagram**

The following seven rules are used to construct data flow diagrams (DFD):

- Arrows should not cross each other.
- Squares, circles, and files must bear names.
- Decomposed data flows must be balanced (all data flows on the decomposed diagram must reflect flows in the original diagram).
- No two data flows, squares, or circles can have the same name.
- Draw all data flows around the outside of the diagram.
- Choose meaningful names for data flows, processes, and data stores. Use strong verbs followed by nouns.
- Control information such as record counts, passwords, and validation requirements are not pertinent to a data-flow diagram.

Context DFD

A data flow diagram (DFD) of the scope of an organizational system that shows the system boundaries, external entities that interact with the system and the major information flows between the entities and the system. A context DFD does not show any detail but show an overview drawing of the system. It is an excellent diagram to show all basic parts or functions of a system. Context DFD place a boundary around the system under investigation, saying that this is what will be examined - nothing more and nothing less. After developing a context DFD, you may turn your attention to the details of proposed system.

Level 0 DFD

A data flow diagram (DFD) that represents a system's major processes, data flows and data stores at a high level of detail.

Nested Data Flow Diagram

A data flow diagram is used to represent the high level functionality of a system, that can be further divided into smaller functional units. A process can be expanded into another data flow diagram. Each input and output of a process will become next input or output for next data flow diagram. In nested data flow diagram you can show data store, that is not visible in high level diagram. Like a tree structure in nested data flow diagram you can have many levels of depth.

3.5 FUNCTIONAL CONSTRAINTS

Functional constraints are functional relationship between entities of an object model. The term entity includes objects, classes, attributes, link and associations. A constraints is used to restrict the values that entities can consume like no students will get marks more than 100 or no employee will get bonus more than 5000 etc. Using functional constraints you can set validations on your entities.

3.6 SAMPLE FUNCTIONAL MODEL (CURRENCY EXCHANGE CONTROL SYSTEM)

The Currency Control System is a Software program that interacts with currency control equipment to store and exchange various international currencies, a user will input currency in one form and machine will convert it in another form.

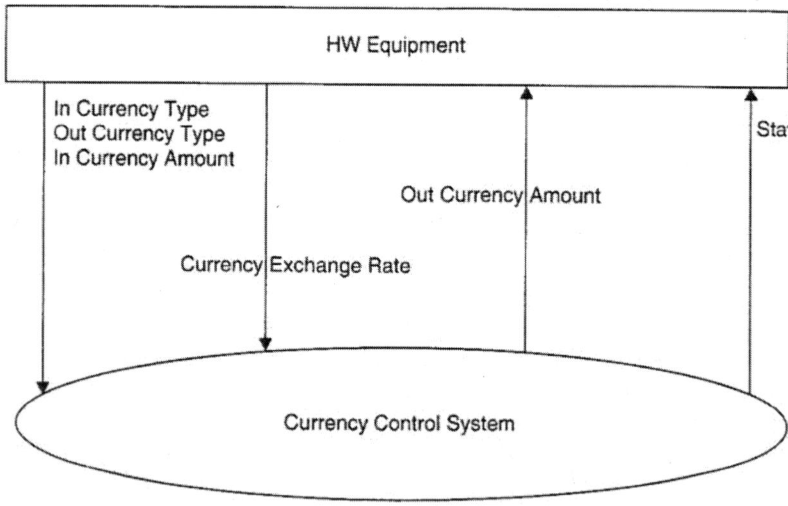

FIGURE 3.3 **Context level Data flow diagram of currency control system**

The basic transformation in the exchange Currency system operation will be to compute an Out Currency Amount based upon an In Currency Amount, In Currency Type, and Out Currency Type. The basic transformation is:

Out Currency Amount = In Currency Amount * currencyRates [In Currency Type]

Correctness assertions must be identified to ensure that correct outAmount should be computed.

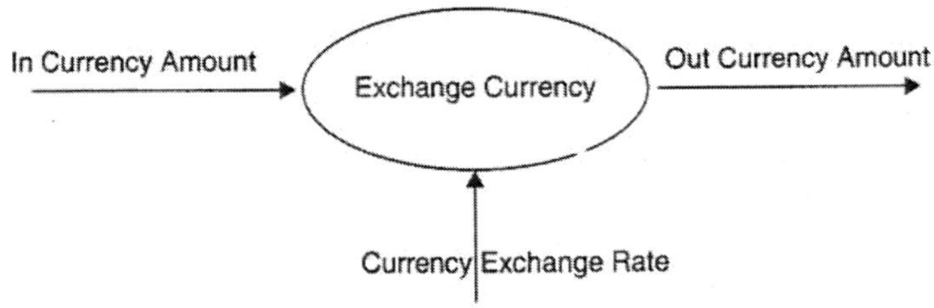

FIGURE 3.4 **Data flow diagram of exchange currency control system**

REVIEW QUESTIONS

1. Describe various symbols used in data flow diagram alongwith their significance. **(UTU-2002)**
2. Write in brief about Nested dataflow diagram, Functional constraints. **(UTU-2002)**
3. Discuss various ways to implement DFD's. Prepare a dataflow diagram for computing the roots of the equation $ax^2 + bx + c = 0$. Inputs are a, b and c, outputs are R1, R2. That may be real or complex depend upon inputs. **(UTU-2003)**
4. Describe the relation of functional model to object and dynamic model. **(UTU-2003, 2005)**
5. Prepare a dataflow diagram for computing the volume and surface area of a cylinder. Inputs are height and radius and outputs are volume and surface area. Discuss various ways to implement the DFD. **(UTU-2004)**
6. Prepare a DFD for the payroll system in a company. **(UTU-2004)**
7. Explain the following with reference to Data flow diagrams - Actors, Data stores, Control flows. **(UTU-2005)**

Chapter 4 OMT METHODOLOGIES

4.1 FROM OBJECT-ORIENTED DESIGN TO IMPLEMENTATION

In previous chapters you have learn how to model a small system, when you have some familiarity with basic Object oriented concepts, documentation products, and CASE tools. In this section you will learn how you can implement your model of system after design, or how to model and prototype a big system of classes. You need to apply the basic Object-Oriented concepts as listed below:

Object-Oriented Entities - system environment, system, interacting system, class and object

Object-Oriented Relationships - association, aggregation, generalization specialization, interaction (events and messages)

Models - system object model, system dynamic model, system functional model, object model, dynamic model, functional model

Documentation Products - diagrams, text specifications, code

Tools - Windows CASE tools, Windows drawing tool, Windows word processor, Windows C++ Compiler etc.

Object-Oriented modeling follows the Analysis Model of OMT Object -Oriented methodology with interpretations. Object -Oriented modeling emphasizes the early identification of the system environment and the identification of separate interface, control, and entity classes for highly portable systems. You should follow an iterative approach to model and prototype a system. First learn a system level point of view to model the system as a whole. You can take example of a TV Control System from a system point of view and create the system object model, system dynamic model, and the system functional model. Then you should think about inside the TV Control System and identify classes, attributes, operations, relationships, etc. After doing all that things you can create the object model, dynamic model, and functional model.

Following steps will help you to proper implementation of OMT mythologies on a system:

Trace Key Modeling Entities

There can be several key entities in modeling the system within its environment. These can be defined as:

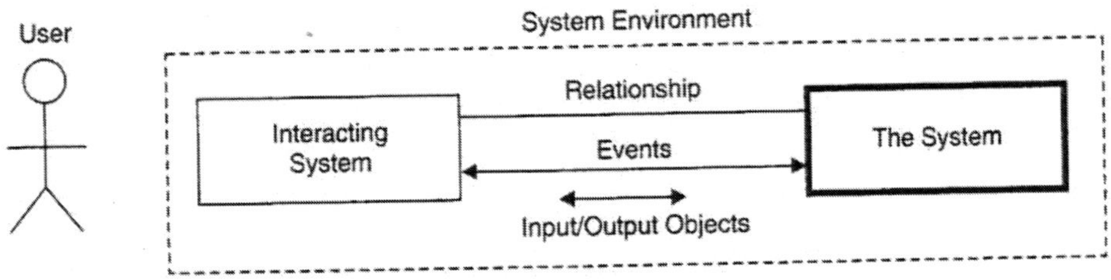

FIGURE 4.1 **System with Interacting Systems**

User- A user is a human, a machine, or other entity that interacts with the system environment to change or receive benefit from the system. For example, a user of a word processing program is the person sending a print command to the word processor to print a document. A user of an air traffic control system is the human air traffic controller. A user may have a **use case** which is the sequence of interactions for a typical use of the system. For example, a typical use case for a bank automatic teller machine is "withdraw cash".

System Environment - The system environment consists of a system and interacting systems (devices or programs). In Software, GUI based text processor is a system environment with a system, for example, the text processor program and interacting systems (device or program), for example, a GUI system and a file system.

System - The system is the system to be modeled and prototyped. It is our center of focus. It generally consists of 10 to 100 classes as a rough order of magnitude. It is generally programmed as a single .EXE or concurrent process. The text editor program is an example of a system. A large system may be partitioned into subsystems. A subsystem may consist of other subsystems or the subsystem may consist of classes. A system may have **system attributes** which are a characteristic or property of the system as a whole. A system has **system operations** which are major functions, activities, or services that the system performs.

Interacting System (Device Or Program) - An interacting system (device or program) is any entity that interacts with the system. An interacting system can be a Hardware device, Software program, a GUI program, a data management program, a communications program, etc. An interacting system is sometimes called an actor, terminator, outside agent, or external system.

Input and Output Object - An input object and output object are objects that are passed as a parameter in an input event and or an output event. It exists in the system environment and is manipulated by the system. Examples are bank account, customer, registration, product, etc. that are passed into or from the system. An input or output object is sometimes called a real world object, a domain object, or problem domain object.

Trace Key Modeling Relationships

Relationships - A system has a relationship with one or more interacting systems. A system is associated ("has a", "knows about", "is associated with") with one or more interacting systems. A system interacts with one or more interacting systems with input and output events. These are defined below.

Association Relationship - An association relationship is a connection or link between the system and an interacting system. In an association relationship the system has one of the following with an interacting system:

- the system "has a" interacting system,
- the system "knows about" an interacting system,
- the system "is associated with" an interacting system.

Interaction Relationship (Events) - An interaction relationship is a communication, interaction, or stimulus response connection between the system and an interacting system. In an interaction relationship, there are one or more input or output events between the system and an interacting system.

Input Event - An input event is a stimulus (interaction or communication) from an interacting system (device or program) to the system. The system must detect and respond. An input event is based on a user or physical phenomenon such as a user action of pressing a function key. Examples of input events are turn on, turn off, record data, store data, print report, etc. Generally, a menu item or button in a GUI window represents an input event. The input event represent the functional requirements of the system, *i.e.*, what the system must do. In implementation, an input event could be a message, remote procedure call, interrupt, or other communication.

Output Event - An output event is an outgoing stimulus from the system to an interacting system (device or program). It is in response to an input event such as a message to a printer. Examples of output events to an interacting GUI system are open window, show dialog box, display text, etc. Examples of output events to an interacting data base management system are get record, update record, delete record, find record, etc. In implementation, an output event could be a message, remote procedure call, or other communication.

Trace Key Patterns

To rapidly model and prototype Object Oriented systems, it is desirable to understand the basic patterns, structures, and architectures in the systems we're working on. In the real world we see patterns, structures, and architectures all around us. We see houses, buildings, tables, chairs, stairs, etc. In Windows operating system we see windows, dialog boxes, lists. Each of these represent a well defined pattern, structure, or architecture. The term pattern is the broadest and most general term describing a high level entity, like a group of entities that work together to perform a function.

Create the System Requirements Statement

The purpose of the system requirements statement is to state the system requirements for the system. The system requirements statement is a primary document to describe the system requirements and functions of the system. The system requirements statement is the problem statement and charter. The emphasis in the system requirements statement is to describe the system and its interactions with interacting systems (devices or programs). For simple systems, the system requirements statement consists of a few sentences stating what the system must do. For complex systems, the system requirements statement may be thousands of pages of detailed requirements and specifications.

The TV Control System is a software program or system that receives commands (input events) from a TV Buttons Device (interacting system) and sends commands (output events) to TV Speaker Device, TV Channel Device, and TV Storage Device (interacting systems). The TV Control System stores the last used volume and channel selection. The commands (input events) are turn on, turn off, increase volume, decrease volume, increase channel, and decrease channel. The TV

Control System initiates the following output events: retrieve volume, store volume, set volume, retrieve channel, store channel, and set channel. The following data (input and output objects) are passed in the output events: volume setting and channel setting. The all above lines are part of a system requirement statement of a TV control system.

Create the System Drawings

The purpose of the system drawing is to provide a physical, real world view of the system environment including the user, Hardware devices, Software programs, etc. A drawing is a physical diagram of the system environment showing typical users, hardware devices, software programs, and input and output objects passed into and from the system.

The following are the steps to create the system drawing:

Step 1. Show the system as a box in the middle of the system drawing.

Step 2. Show users and their user roles, *e.g.*, user, operator, etc.

Step 3. Show the interacting systems (H/W devices and S/W programs) that interact with the system.

Step 4. Show the association between the system and interacting systems (H/W devices and S/W programs).

Step 5. Optionally, draw small arrow symbols to represent input and output objects that are passed to and from the system in events.

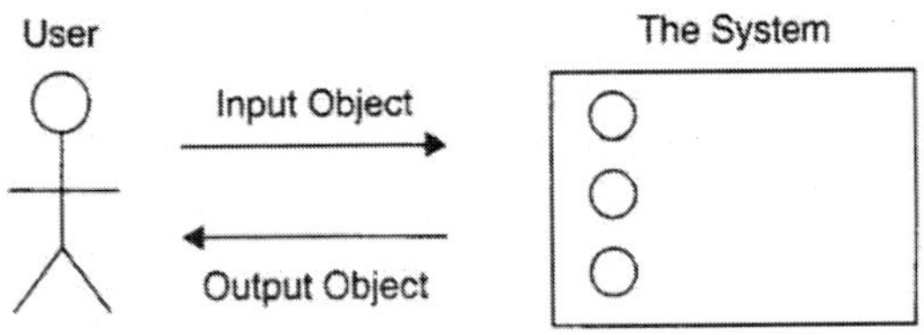

FIGURE 4.2 **System Drawing**

Creating the System Block Diagram

The system block diagram shows a high level view of the system environment with the system and interacting systems (devices or programs). The system block diagram has boxes for each major entity in the system environment. It shows major hardware devices, software programs, and relationships. This section describes the system block diagram including its purpose, steps to create, and a sample block diagram.

The system block diagram shows the system being modeled and interacting systems (devices or programs) within the system environment. The system block diagram shows interacting systems that initiate commands (input events). The system block diagram show interacting systems that receive responses (output events). An input object is passed into the system. An output object is passed from the system. The system block diagram leads to the system interaction diagram (events).

The purpose of the system block diagram is to show the system, interacting systems (also called terminators, actors, or agents), input objects (also known as input data flows), and output objects (also known as output data flows). The input and output objects may be an atomic object, a structured object, and a collection object. The system block diagram is a graphic, visual representation showing the system inputs and outputs (objects) with interacting systems. The system block diagram has a box for the system being modeled and a box for each interacting system. Input and output objects are shown as small arrows. The system block diagram is functionally equivalent to the Structured Analysis system context diagram.

Creating OMT Class Diagram Notation

The steps to create the system diagram (OMT Class Diagram Notation) are:

Step 1. Start with the system block diagram showing the system and interacting systems.

Step 2. Place an OMT class symbol in the middle of the page to represent the system.

Step 3. For each interacting system, place an OMT class symbol on the page. Show an association between the system and the interacting system.

Step 4. Fill in the **system attributes**. A system attribute is a property or characteristic of the system. Ask the question, "As a system, what objects or data do I know about?"

Step 5. Fill in the **system operations**. A system operation is a function or transformation of the system as a whole. Ask the questions, "As a system, what do I do?" "As a system, what are my major functions?" "As a system, what input events do I respond to?"

Step 6. For each interacting system, fill in the system attributes and system operations. The system has a system operation for each input event. An interacting system that receives output events has a system operation for each output event.

Creating the Data Dictionary

The data dictionary lists the terms used in the system and a brief description of each term. In the system object model, the data dictionary lists the system and the interacting systems. Additionally, it may list the system attributes and system operations.

Modeling System Events and States

The purpose of the system dynamic model is to show stimulus response behavior over time of a system. The system dynamic model corresponds to the OMT Dynamic Model at the system level. In the system dynamic model, we define stimulus response behavior and the time oriented sequence (scenario) of input and output events. We define the states, e.g. modes of behavior of the system.

Creating the Use Case Diagram

The use case diagram and descriptions are useful to capture requirements. A general use case diagram is shown in Figure 4.3.

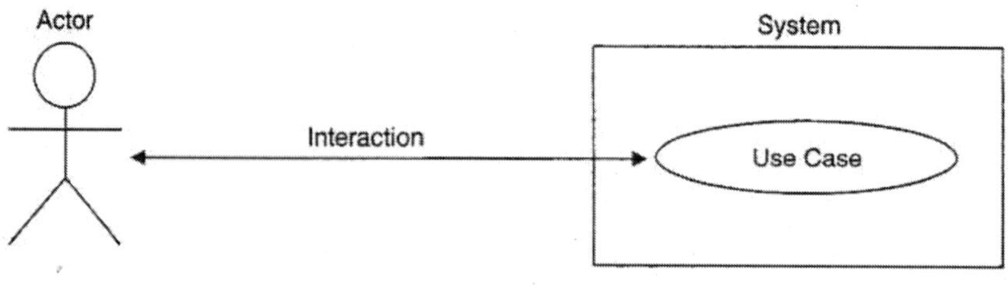

FIGURE 4.3 **Use Case Diagram**

The steps to create the use case diagram and descriptions are:

Step 1. Start with the requirements statement.

Step 2. Identify the actors, use cases, sub-use cases. Describe each use case in terms of the sequence of input and output events.

Step 3. Create the use case diagram and use case table.

Step 4. Walk through the use case diagram.

Creating the System Interaction Diagram

The purpose of the system interaction diagram (events) is to show the scope and boundary of the system in terms of input and output events. The system interaction diagram (events) displays the system, input events, and output events in graphic form.

Both the system interaction diagram (events) and structured analysis context diagram set the boundary of the system.

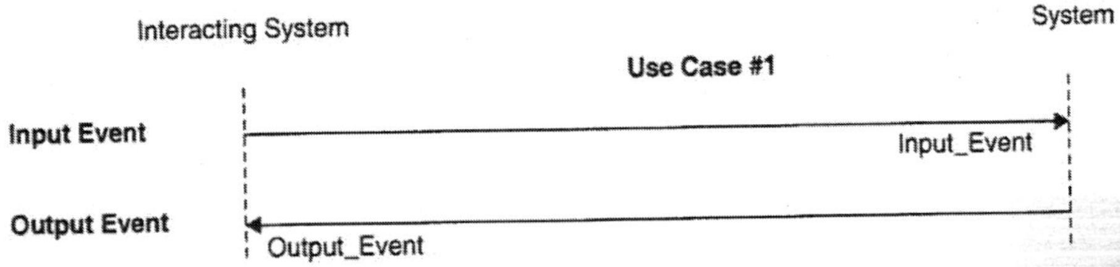

FIGURE 4.4 **System interaction diagram**

Creating the System State Diagram

The purpose of the system state diagram is to show the stimulus response behavior of a system in terms of input events, conditions, states, and output events. The system state diagram (state transition diagram) specifies stimulus response logic for a system. It specifies the pattern of input events, conditions, actions, and states.

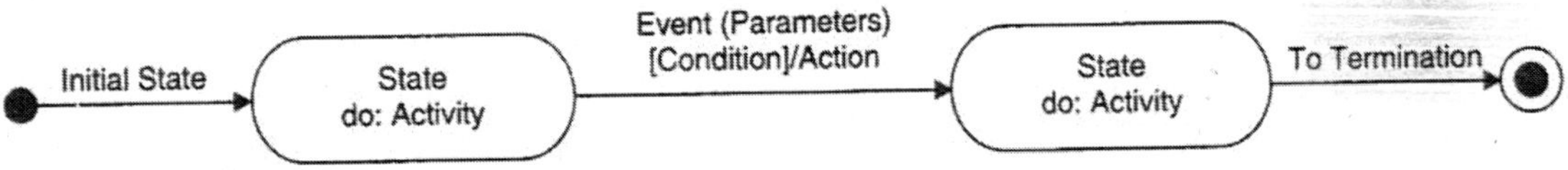

FIGURE 4.5 **System state diagram**

Modeling the System Inputs, Outputs, and Operations

The purpose of the system functional model is to describe transformations (operations) and input and output objects for the system as a whole. The system functional model corresponds to the OMT Functional Model at the system level. We identify the input objects and output objects for the system as a whole. We identify system operations. The system operations represent the system's behavior. Transformations occur in the system operations. As shown below, a system operation may have preconditions, postconditions, and exceptions.

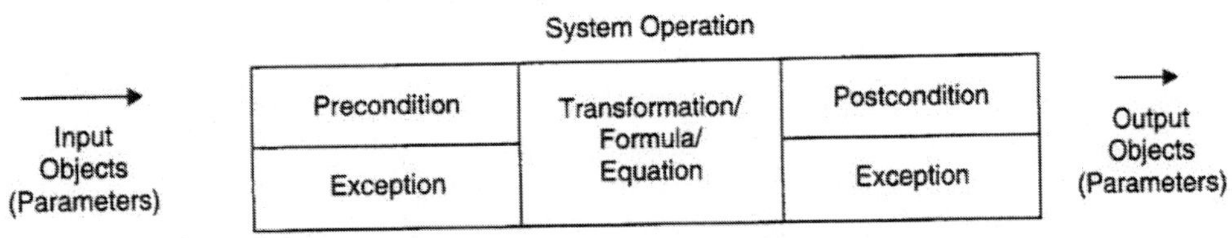

FIGURE 4.6 **System functional model diagram**

4.2 OMT METHODOLOGIES

An object-oriented methodology has a defined set of entities like system, class, object, graphic symbols, diagrams, forms, rules, and procedures. It is a process that generally covers the entire software lifecycle from requirements to implementation phase to develop a quality software. Many CASE tool supports a subset graphic notation for several object-oriented methodologies, Like:

- Rumbaugh Object Modeling Technique (OMT)
- Coad/Yourdon Object-Oriented Analysis and Design (OOA/OOD)
- Booch Object-Oriented Design (OOD)
- Shlaer Mellor OOA/OOD

Rumbaugh Object Modeling Technique (OMT)

This Object Oriented methodology is documented in *Object-Oriented Modeling and Design* by James Rumbaugh. It has a strong data modeling origin. It has a very comprehensive graphic notation. Analysis in OMT consists of the Object Model, Dynamic Model, and Functional Model which has been discussed earlier. Analysis is followed by system design and detailed design are main part of OMT.

Coad/Yourdon Object-Oriented Analysis and Design (OOA/OOD)

This Object Oriented methodology is documented in *Object-Oriented Analysis* and *Object-Oriented Design* by Peter Coad and Ed Yourdon [Coad-91a and Coad-91b]. It has a strong data modeling origin. It has a simple graphic notation. OOA consists of identifying and organizing classes from different points of view called layers. OOD consists of refining the OOA model for the human interface, problem domain, data management, and concurrent task management.

Booch Object-Oriented Design (OOD)

This Object Oriented methodology is documented in *Object-Oriented Design with Applications* by Grady Booch [Booch-94]. It has a very strong real-time and message passing origin. It has an extensive, comprehensive graphic notation. OOD consists of modeling a system by identifying, organizing, and specifying subsystems, classes, objects, implementation modules and processes.

Shlaer Mellor OOA/OOD

This Object Oriented methodology is documented in *Object Lifecycles - Modeling the World in States* by Sally Shlaer and Stephen Mellor [Shlaer-92]. OOA consists of information (data) models, state models, and process models similar to the OMT object model, dynamic model, and functional model. OOD consists of refining the OOA models for an implementation environment.

4.3 STRUCTURED SYSTEMS ANALYSIS AND DESIGN(SA/SD)

Structured Systems Analysis and Design Method (SA/SD) is a systems approach to the analysis and design of information systems. SA/SD was produced for the CCTA, a UK government office concerned with the use of technology in government. System design methods are a discipline within the software development industry which seek to **provide a framework for activity and the capture, storage, transformation and dissemination of information so as to enable the economic development** of computer systems that are fit for purpose. SA/SD is a waterfall method by which an Information System design can be arrived. SA/SD can be thought to represent a pinnacle of the rigorous document-led approach to system design, and contrasts with more contemporary Rapid Application Development methods such as DSDM.

- "Structured analysis and design is a set of techniques and graphical tools that allow the analyst to develop a new kind of system specification that are easily understandable to the user. Analysts work primarily with their wits, pencil and paper." [Kendall 1996]
- "[The purpose of SASD] is to develop a useful, high quality information system that will meet the needs of the end user." [Yourdon, 1989]

SA/SD is Developed in the late 1970s by DeMarco, Yourdon, and Constantine after the emergence of structured programming. IBM incorporated SA/SD into their development cycle in the late 1970s and early 1980s. Classical SA/SD was modified due to its inability to represent real-time systems. In 1989, Yourdon published "Modern Structured Analysis".

Philosophy of Structured Analysis and Design

- You can attempt to divide large, complex problems into smaller, more easily known as "Divide and Conquer".
- There can be Top-Down approach if you go through Classical SA, or Middle-Out in case of Modern SA.
- You can design the system using a functional view of the problem.
- You can use graphics to illustrate their ideas whenever possible.
- You can keep written record if form of Software requirements specifications.

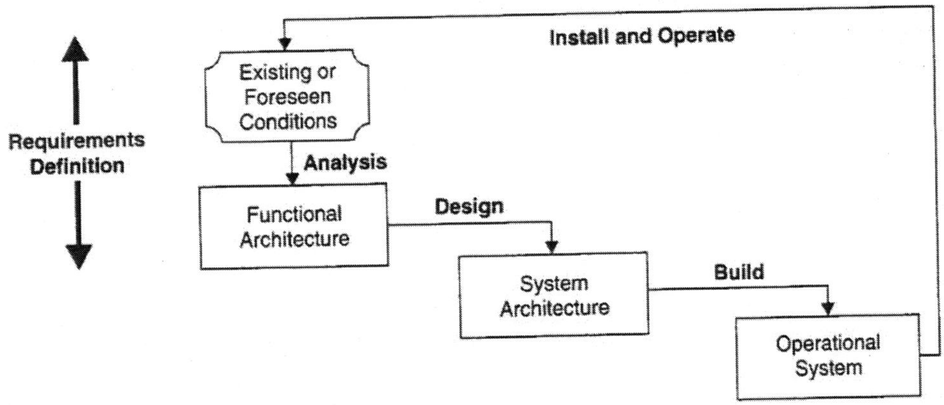

FIGURE 4.7 **Structured systems analysis and design**

Parts of SA/SD Model

- **The Environmental Model**
  - Statement of Purpose
  - Context Diagram
  - Event List
- **The Behavioural Model**
  - Data Flow Diagram
  - Process Specification

- Data Dictionary
- Entity-Relationship Diagram

- **The Implementation Model:**
  - Structure Diagram

4.4 SA/SD Vs OOAD

Similarities

- Both SASD and OOAD had started off from programming techniques.
- Both techniques use graphical design and graphical tools to analyze and model the requirements.
- Both techniques provide a systematic step-by-step process for developers.
- Both techniques focus on documentation of the requirements.

Differences

- SASD is Process-Oriented.
- OOAD is Data-Oriented.
- Another difference is that OOAD encapsulates as much of the systems' data and processes into objects.
- while SASD separates between them.

4.5 JACKSON SYSTEM DEVELOPMENT (JSD)

Jackson System Development is a method for specifying and designing systems, in which the factor of time is significant and they may be described using sequences of events. Michael A. Jackson's design method assumes the design of the system is an extention of the programme design. JSD has been based on the JSP method (Jackson Structured Programming) this is because the techniques used during program developent also apply to developing systems.

There are two main differences between JSD and other system development methods. The first is that the initial area of interest for JSD is the domain of the software, not the software itself. Secondly, the method is focused on event sequencing. The domain is the set of real world events, which sequentially ordered in time. JSD was described in Jackson's book System Development (1983) and in the collection of articles JSP and JSD, edited by John Cameron (1989). JSD was the first "object-oriented" system design method, as its basic conception of a computer system was as a network of communicating sequential processes (objects).

Way of working

The basic principle of operation of JSD is that development must start with describing and modeling the real world, rather than specifying or structuring the function performed by the system. A system made using JSD method performs the simulation of the real world before any direct attention is paid to function or purpose of the system. The second principle states, that an adequate model of a time-ordered world must itself be time-ordered. Main aim is to map progress in the real world on progress in the system that models it. The third principle is that the way of implementing the system is based on transformation of specification into efficient set of processes. These processes should be designed in such a manner that it would be possible to run them on available software and hardware. When it was originally presented by Jackson in 1983, the method consisted of six steps:

1. Entity/Action Step
2. Initial Model Step
3. Interactive Function Step
4. Information Function Step
5. System Timing Step
6. System Implementation Step

After combining some steps there will be only three steps:

1. Modeling Stage (Analysis). In the modeling stage the developers make a description of the aspects of the business or organization that the system will be concerned with. To make this a description they must analyze their business, choosing what is relevant and ignoring what is not. They have to consider the organization as it will be, not as it is now. The model description is written very precisely. This precision forces the developer to ask detailed questions. It encourages good communication and understanding between developers, users, and everyone else involved with the new system. The model description consists of actions, entities and related information. An action is an event, usually in the external reality, that is relevant to the system and whose occurrence the system must record. In implementation terms, actions might cause database updates. We start Jackson System Development by making a list of actions with definitions and associated attributes. Diagrams describe ordering relationships between actions. The diagrams describe the entities, people or, things that the system is concerned with. The data that is to be stored for each entity is then defined. In effect we are choosing what is to be remembered by each entity about the actions that affect it. The full definition of this data includes an elaboration of the entity diagram to show in detail the update rules.

2. Network Stage (Design). In the network stage we build up a precise description of what the system has to do, including the outputs that are to be produced and the way the system is to appear to the user. This description is in terms of a network of programs. More precisely, it is a network of Communicating Sequential Processes (CSP), a concept developed by Tony Haoare. You will start this network by making one program for each of the entities that was defined during the modeling stage. The network is then built up incrementally by adding new programs and connecting them up to the existing network. New programs are added for the following reasons:

- To collect inputs for actions, check them for errors, and pass them to the entity programs. In this way entity programs are kept up-to-date with what's happening outside;
- To generate inputs for actions that do not correspond to external events. Such actions are substitutes for real world events, perhaps because those events cannot be detected;
- To calculate and produce outputs.

There are two means of connecting programs in the network. These are by data streams (represented on our network diagram of circles) and by state vector inspection (represented on our network diagrams by diamonds). Whatever kind of connection is appropriate, the entity programs play a pivotal role in the construction of the network. Most of the new programs can be connected directly to the entity programs.

You will then draw a whole set of network diagrams to describe the system. Different networks usually only have entity programs in common. The complete system is represented by the overlay of all the diagrams.

The diagrams are supported by textual information describing the contents of the data streams and state vector connections. The new programs that are added to the network are defined using the same diagrammatic notation used to describe the ordering of actions. These new programs are designed using the JSP (Jackson Structured Programming) method, which is now a subset of JSD.

3. Implementation Stage (Realisation). The result of the implementation stage is the final system. This stage is the only one directly concerned with the machine and the associated software on which the system is to run. Therefore, as well as producing and testing code, the implementation stage covers physical design issues. In particular it covers:

- physical data design, and
- reconfiguring the network by combining programs.

Physical data design is about the design of files or databases. The details of database design depend on the particular DBMS being used. However, the necessary information about the application is all available from the network stage. The most important is the data defined for each entity and the high volume accessing of that data as defined by the frequently used state vector connections.

4.6 EXAMPLES / CASE STUDIES

Student Loan System

A university gives loans to students. Before getting a loan, there is an evaluation process after which agreement is always reached. A TE transaction records each step of the evaluation process, and a TA transaction records the overall loan agreement. A student can take any number of loans, but only one can be active at any time. Each loan is initiated by a TI transaction. Then, the student repays the loan with a series of repayments. Each repayment transaction is recorded by a TR transaction. Finally, a loan is terminated by a TT transaction.

Two output functions are desired: (1) an inquiry function that prints out the loan balance for any student, and (2) a repayment acknowledgment sent to each student after payment is received by the university.

SOLUTION

Modeling Phase

JSD consists of three main phases:

The modeling phase; the network phase; and the implementation phase. First of all start with the modeling phase. The modeling phase consists of three steps:

Step 1: Entity/action step

Actions have the following characteristics:

1. An action takes place at a point in time
2. An action must take place in the real world outside of the system.
3. An action is atomic, cannot be divided into subactions.

Entities have the following characteristics:

1. An entity performs or suffers actions in time.
2. An entity must exist in the real world, and not be a construct of a system that models the real world.
3. An entity must be capable of being regarded as an individual; and, if there are many entities of the same type, of being uniquely named.

Here are the candidate lists:

Entities/Description:

student

system

university

loan

student-loan

Actions/Attributes:

evaluate - action of university? (university performs the evaluation); action of student? (student is evaluated)

attributes: student-id, loan-no, date of evaluation, remarks

agree - action of university? (university agrees to loan); action of student? (agrees to loan)

attributes: student-id, loan-no, date of agreement, amount of loan, interest rate, repayment period)

make loan - action of university

attributes: student-id, loan-no, date of loan, loan amount, interest rate, repayment period

initiate - action of university? (university initiates loan); action of student? (student initiates loan); action of loan? (is initiated)

attributes: student-id, date initiated

repay - action of loan? (loan is repaid); action of student? (student repays the loan);

attributes: student-id, date of repayment, amount of repayment

terminate - action of loan (loan is terminated);

attributes: student-id, date of termination, remarks

After discussion and reflection, you end up with the following entity and action lists:

Entities/Description:

student

Actions/Attributes:

evaluate - action of student; student? (student suffers the action, is evaluated);

attributes: student-id, loan-no, date of evaluation, remarks

agree - action of student

attributes: student-id, loan-no, date of agreement, amount of loan, interest rate, repayment period) initiate - action of student

attributes: student-id, date initiated

repay - action of student

attributes: student-id, date of repayment, amount of repayment

terminate - action of student

attributes: student-id, date of termination, remarks

Step 2: Entity structure step

The behavior of an entity in the real-world is modeled in terms of the actions it performs or suffers over time. The second step of JSD expresses the constraints in the ordering of an entity actions with a structure diagram.

The entity structure diagram for a student is shown below:

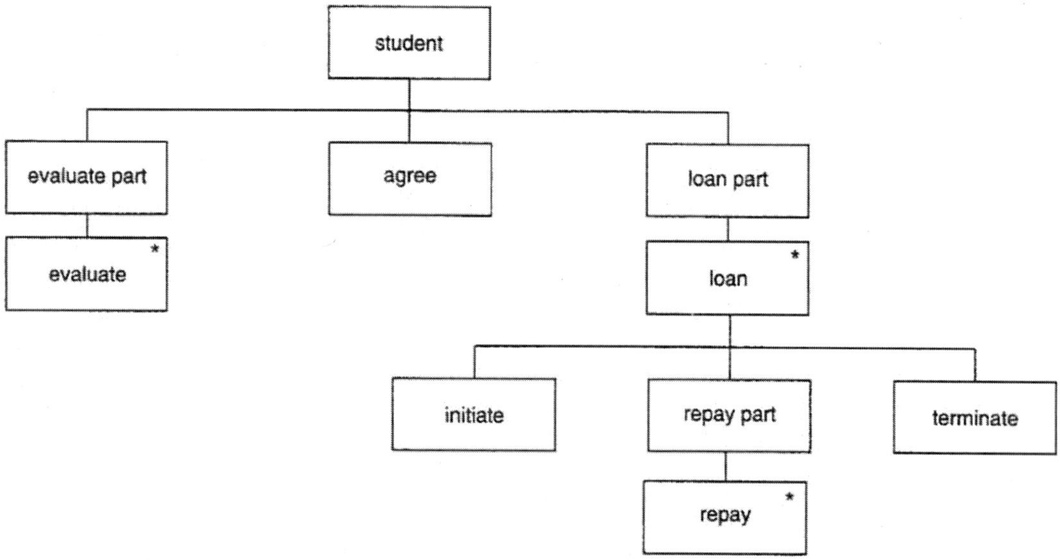

Step 3: Model process step

In the last step of the modeling phase we create an executable **model process** for each entity in the system. Each model process is described with a system diagram.

Our information system models each real-world entity. We are not just simulating entities artificially, using some statistical techniques for example; we are modeling each entity precisely as it exists in the real world. Therefore, there must be a connection between the entity in the real world and the entity model process in our information system.

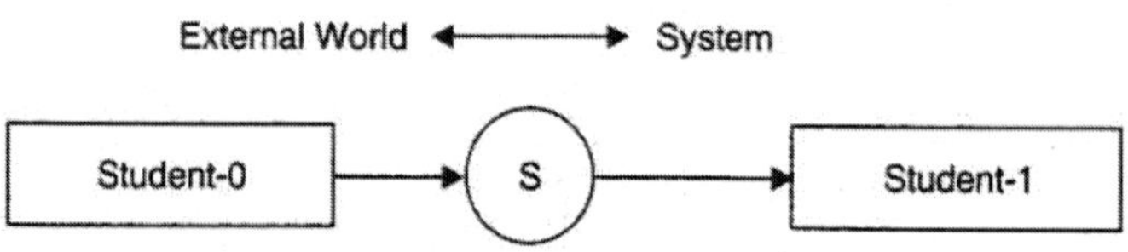

use the suffix "-0" to the student entity to indicate the abstract student entity in the real world, and the suffix "-1" to indicate the realization of this abstraction in our information system.

Network Phase

In the network phase, we connect model processes and functions in a single system specification diagram (SSD). In our system, we have one entity and two functions. The SSD is shown below:

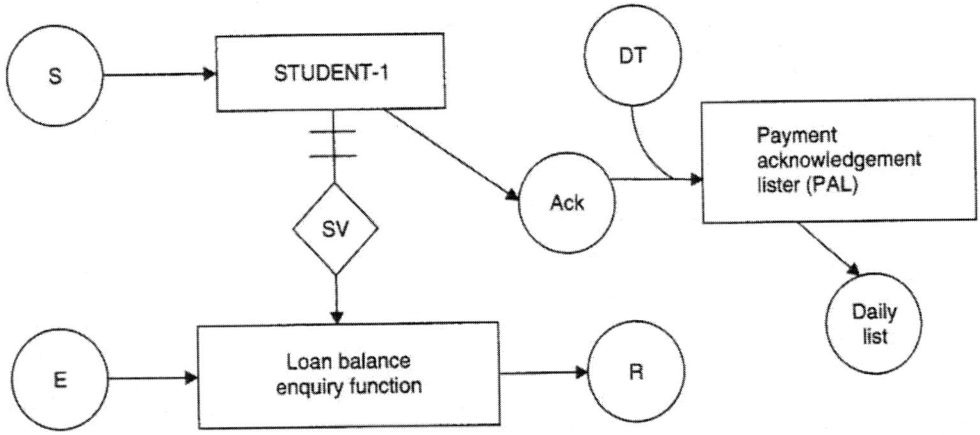

The loan balance inquiry function (LBE) is connected to the Student-1 process by state vector (SV) connection. In this type of connection, one process can examine the state vector of a second process. The double lines indicate that an inquiry process, over its life, will examine many student processes.

The function to produce the student acknowledgments data stream (ACK) is embedded in the student-1 process in the repays component as shown below:

DT is an input signal at the end of the day—a daily time marker—that tells the payment acknowledgment lister (PAL) function to begin. The ACK and DT data streams are rough-merged, that is, we don't know precisely whether a repayment acknowledgment will appear on today's or tomorrow's daily list.

The loan balance inquiry function (LBE) is designed using JSP as shown below:

(*i*) input and output data structures:

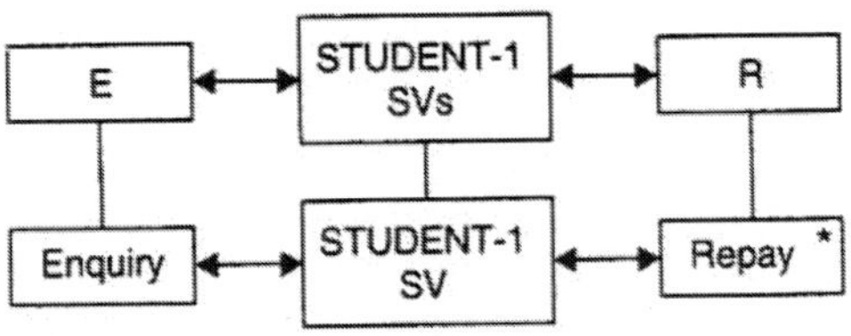

(*ii*) basic program structure:

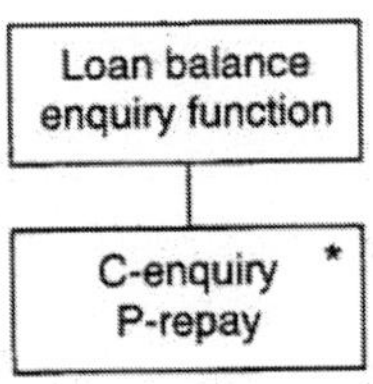

(*iii*) list of operations:

1. write 'loan balance for', student-id, 'is', balance
2. get STUDENT SV (student-id)
3. read E

(*iv*) elaborated program structure and text:

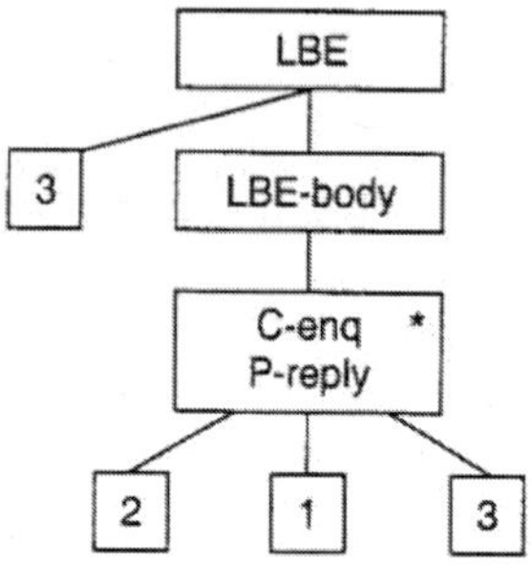


```
LBE     seq

  read E;
  LBE-BODY itr     (forever)
     get STUDENTSV(student-id);
     write 'loan balance for', stud ent-id,
        'is', balance
     read E;
  LBE-BODY   end
LBE  end
```

Implementation Phase

First we examine the timing constraints of the system. The problem description for our system states that inquiries are to be answered on-line but repayment acknowledgments at the end of the day.

We then consider possible hardware and software for implementing our system. We decide to implement all student processes on a single processor. Each student process could have been allocated a dedicated processor. Based on hardware and timing constraints, we design a system implementation diagram (SID) shown below:

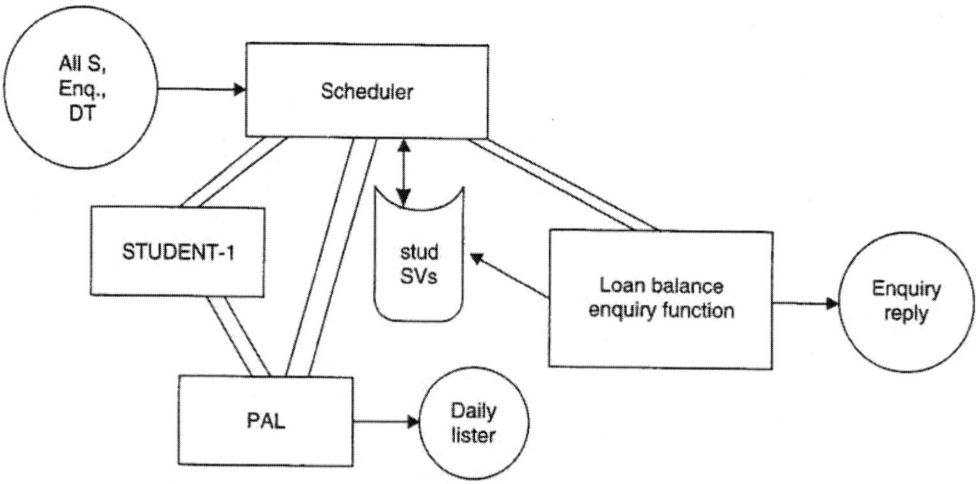

In the SID, all of the serial data streams are input to the scheduler process. Note that the all student processes have an identical structure text; only their state vectors are different. Consequently, we can separate the state vectors of student processes from their process text—this separation is called state vector separation. The set of state vectors constitutes the data base of our student loan system.

The student-1 process is inverted with respect to its data stream, S. Student-1 is called by the scheduler to process a transaction, and then suspended when it has completed the processing of the transaction, with control returning to the scheduler. Note that the scheduler must access the student's state vector corresponding to the student-id on the input data stream, and for saving the updated state vector on completion of processing the transaction.

The loan balance inquiry is invoked by the scheduler when it has read an inquiry.

The repayment acknowledgment Lister (PAL) is inverted with respect to both of its inputs, the repayment acknowledgment data stream and the daily marker. PAL is invoked by Student-1 whenever Student-1 processes a repayment transaction. The scheduler invokes PAL directly when it receives a DT and this triggers the daily listing.

The scheduler process is designed with JSP, and is shown below:

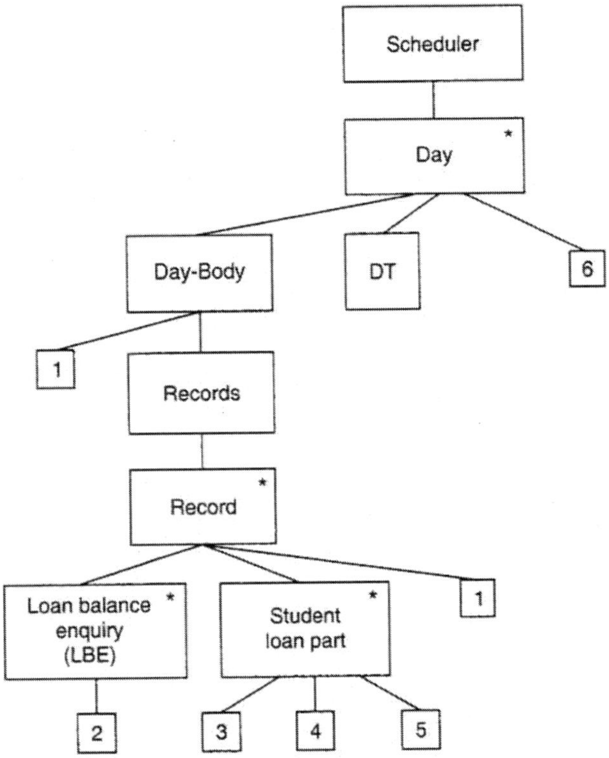

List of operations:

1-read input
2-call LBE(inrec)
3-get SSV(student-id)
4-call student-1(srec, ssv)
5-put SSV(student-id)
6-call PAL(DT)

The exact meaning of the scheduler structure diagram is as follows: On any given day, records from the serial data stream (loan balance inquiries and student loan transactions) are read and processed in real-time. At the end of the day, a daily time marker—perhaps a signal to the system from the operator—is input, and the payment acknowledgment lister program is invoked. It processes payment acknowledgments that have been previously generated in real-time whenever a student repayment is made and stored in a buffer.

REVIEW QUESTIONS

1. Differentiate between JSD and OMT approaches of Software Engineering. **(UTU 2002)**
2. Differentiate between JSD and SA/SD approaches of System development. **(UTU-2003)**
3. Write short notes on JSD and SA/SD. **(UTU-2005)**

Part - B

C++

Chapter 1

OBJECT-ORIENTED MODEL

1.1 HISTORY OF C++

In Early days of computer programming, programmers worked with the most primitive computer instructions say machine language. These instructions were represented by long strings of ones and zeroes. Soon, assemblers were invented to map machine instructions to human-readable and -manageable mnemonics, such as ADD and MOV. Mean time, higher-level languages evolved, such as BASIC, COBOL, C. These languages allow people to work with something approximating words and sentences, such as I = S + 100. These instructions were translated back into machine language by interpreters and compilers. Most of the procedural languages like C was not able to *solve real world problems* using an entity as object and software development process was costly too. As object-oriented analysis, design, and programming began to attract the software industry, Bjarne Stroustrup took the most popular language for commercial software development, C++, and extended it to provide the features needed to facilitate object-oriented programming. He created C++, and in less than a decade it has gone from being used by only a handful of developers at AT&T to being the programming language of choice for an estimated one million developers worldwide soon. Now C++ is a predominant language for commercial software development. While it is true that C++ is a superset of C, and that virtually any legal C program is a legal C++ program, the leap from C to C++ is very significant. C++ benefited from its relationship to C for many years, as C programmers can easily start programming in C++.

1.2 PROCEDURAL Vs OBJECT-ORIENTED PROGRAMMING

Before the invention of C or C++, computer programs were thought of as a series of procedures that acted upon data. In a program a procedure, or a function, can be used as a set of specific instructions executed one after the other. The data was quite separate from the procedures, and the trick in programming was to keep track of which functions called which other functions, and what data values were changed. To make sense of this potentially confusing situation, structured programming was created. The principle idea behind structured programming is as simple as the idea of divide a big task into smaller sub tasks. A computer program can be thought of as consisting of a set of sub tasks. Any task that is too complex to be described simply would be broken down into a set of smaller component tasks, until the tasks were sufficiently small and self-contained enough that they were easily understood. That is also known as top down approach of programming.

Old programs forced the user to proceed step-by-step through a series of screens. Modern event-driven programs like programs of Microsoft Windows present all the choices at once and respond to the user's actions like click or button pressed. Object-oriented programming attempts to respond to these needs, providing techniques for managing enormous complexity, achieving reuse of software components, and coupling data with the tasks that manipulate that data. The essence of object-oriented programming is to treat data and the procedures in a same module known as class. A class can be reuse by many objects at a time that cut the cost of software development.

1.3 FEATURES OF AN OBJECT-ORIENTED PROGRAMMING LANGUAGE

Any object-oriented programming follow the given features of object-oriented development model:

1. Encapsulation
2. Data hiding
3. Inheritance
4. Polymorphism
5. Dynamic Binding.

1. **Encapsulation:** The property of being a self-contained unit is known as encapsulation. Just like a birthday gift, which you will get in wrapped or encapsulated form, without open it you cannot say what is in inside it? In same way an object can be a encapsulated form of its class like a command button in your window. In procedural programming like 'C' you have to define data members and operations of data members seperately. Encapsulation provides you a new way to combine data and member functions in a single unit named class. A programmer can also provide data securities to avoid unaothorised access of data values. A class can be reused several times, you can extend the definition of old class to provide a new form to your object(an instance of a base class).
2. **Data hiding:** With encapsulation, one can accomplish data hiding. Data hiding is the highly valued characteristic, that an object can be used without the user knowing or caring how it works internally. Just as you can open a file on your computer without knowing how the hard disk, memory or word processor applichildion works, so using data hiding concept one can use a well-designed object without knowing about its internal data members. C++ supports the properties of encapsulation and data hiding through the creation of user-defined types, called classes.
3. **Inheritance:** C++ supports the idea of reuse of software codes by many users to cut the time and cost in software applichildion development through inheritance. A new version of a software can inherit or reuse the codes of modules of old version like Windows XP,

inherits properties of Windows-2000 and Windows-2000 inherits the properties of windows-98. One can design a new class adding properties of three or four classes like VB.NET is a combination of Visual basic and Java.

4. **Polymorphism:** C++ supports the idea that different objects do "the right thing" through what is called function polymorphism and class polymorphism. Poly means many, and morph means form. Polymorphism refers to the same name taking many forms. In C++ you can declare many functions with a same name like a function name area() can be used to compute area of a circle, rectangle, square, cube etc.

   C++, Java, Smalltalk and C# are most popular object oriented programming languages, you can apply any of given feature in that languages.

1.4 C++ WITHOUT LEARNING C

C++ is a extension of C, but it does not mean that you should learn C first. It is unnecessary to learn C first one can easily start C++ programming because C++ allow you to write code in C style. You can learn C++ without prior experience of C. Even if you have no programming experience of any kind you can be a good C++ programmer.

1.5 SPDLC (SIMPLE PROGRAM DEVELOPMENT LIFE CYCLE)

In any computer program that you write first time, the development cycle should be: Write the source code of your program, compile the source code, link the program, and run it. Unfortunately, almost every program, can and will have errors, or bugs, in the program. Some bugs will cause the compile to fail, some will cause the link to fail, and some will only show up when you run the program. Whatever type of bug you find, you must fix it, and that involves editing your source code, recompiling and re linking, and then re run your program.

REVIEW QUESTIONS

1. What is the difference between procedural vs object oriented programming.
2. What is object oriented model of programming.
3. Explain the features of object oriented programming languages.
4. Why we should write reusable source codes and how C++ is helpful to write reusable codes.
5. What is a class and an object.

Chapter 2 A QUICK START WITH C++

2.1 YOUR FIRST C++ PROGRAM

The first and important requirement to start programming in C++ is a compiler. C++ is a compiler based language, you can install any of available C++ compiler on your working operating system. If you have Microsoft Windows operating system you have to use Borland Turbo C++ compiler. That compiler has an IDE (Integrated Development Environment) interface, an inbuilt editor to type your source code, menu driven command to compile and run or to convert an executable file. A beginner programmer can start writing programs in C++ using following steps:

1. Write your source code in a file, with .CPP extension.
2. Compile the source code into a file with the .OBJ extension.
3. Link your OBJ file with needed C++ libraries to convert executable

PROGRAM 2.1

```
#include <iostream.h> // C++ library file
void main()
    {
    cout << "Hello World!\n";
    }
```

save this program in a file say hello.cpp, compile it and run, you will get Hello World ! on your screen.

2.2 BUGS IN YOUR C++ PROGRAM

In a program errors can occur for any number of reasons. Usually they are a result of some minor error. Your C++ compilers will not only tell you what you did wrong, it will point you to the exact place in your code where you made the mistake and even suggest a solution. The need is to understand the message produced by the compiler, that you will learn by experience. You can see this by intentionally putting an error into your program. Now write a new program say erhello.cpp with given lines of code:

PROGRAM 2.2

```
#include <iostream.h>
    int main()
    {
    cout << "Hello World!\n";
    return 0;
```

you have missed closing } in your program. Now compile it, you will get a message:

erhello.cpp, line 3: Compound statement missing terminating } in function main().

This error tells you the file and line number of the problem, and what the problem is . Note that the error message points you to line 3. The compiler wasn't sure if you intended to put the closing brace before or after the cout statement on line 3. Sometimes the errors just get you to the general vicinity of the problem and you have to use your brain to correct it.

2.3 WHY # INCLUDE

The first character is any C++ program is the # symbol, which is a signal to the preprocessor. Each time you start your compiler, the preprocessor is run. The preprocessor reads through your source code, looking for lines that begin with the pound symbol (#), and acts on those lines before the compiler runs. include is a preprocessor instruction that says, next is a C++ header filename. Find that file and add it with program. The angle brackets around the filename tell the preprocessor to look in all the usual places for this file. If your compiler is set up correctly, the angle brackets will cause the preprocessor to look for the file iostream.h in the directory that holds all the H files for your compiler mainly include directory.

2.4 IOSTREAM.H HEADER FILE

The file iostream.h (Input-Output-Stream) is used by cout or cin in a C++ program, which assists with writing to the screen or to read by a keyboard. So all the reading and writing operations with general Input or Output devices like keyboard and monitor are done by cout and cin. iostream.h has definition of cout and cin that link with your program at runtime. In future you will include many header files like math.h, string.h, dos.h,graphics.h,conio.h etc. in your program. A header file helps you to reuse the predefined functions stored in libraries of C++.

2.5 COMMENTS

A Comments are for the programmer. When the compiler converts the source code to object code, it throws the comments and the white space away. This means that they have no effect on the executable program. Comments do make your source file bigger, but this is usually of little concern. To summarize, you should use comments and white space to make your source code as easy to understand and maintain as possible. The // is a symbol that will start a comment in a C++ program like:

PROGRAM 2.3

```
//my first C++ program
#include <iostream.h> // C++ library file
void main()
    {
    cout << "Hello Amrapalins !\n";
    }
```

You can also use C style coments in a C++ program which are /* and */ symbols.

REVIEW QUESTIONS

1. **What is the difference between the compiler and the preprocessor?**
2. **Why is the function main() special?**
3. **What are the two types of comments, and how do they differ?**
4. **Is it must to use return as a last statement in a C++ program?**
5. **What is void before main?**

LAB EXERCISES

1. **In you lab check the C++ compiler you are using.**
2. **Check the dir settings of your C++ compiler.**
3. **Check the color settings and try to change it.**
4. **Write a program to print "Hello World !" 10 times on screen save it as hello.cpp.**
5. **Write a program to print * on complete screen using cout statement.**
6. **Look at the following program and check output in lab.**

```
#include <iostream.h>
void main0
{
int x = 50;
int y = 17;
cout "\n";
cout << x + y << " " << x * y;
cout "\n";
}
```

7. Type in the program given, compile and run it and correct the error

```
#include <iostream.h>
void main()
{
int dt =25;
int year = 1972;
cout "\n";
cout <<dt<< year;
cout "\n";
}
```

8. Type in the following program and compile it. Check the error

```
include <iostream.h>
int main()
{
cout << "Hello World\n";
}
```

Chapter 3

VARIABLES, DATA TYPES AND TOKENS

3.1 VARIABLES IN C++

A variable is a named data storage location in your computer's memory. By using a variable's name in your program, you can refer a name to data stored value like:

```
int firstnumber = 0;
```

here is firstnumber is a variable which will store an integer value in future.

3.2 RULES FOR VARIABLE NAMES

To use variables in your C++ programs, you must know how to create variable names. In C++, variable names must adhere to the following rules:

1. The name can contain letters, digits, and the underscore character (_).
2. The first character of the name must be a letter. The underscore is also a legal first character, but its use is not recommended.
3. Case matters (that is, upper- and lowercase letters). Thus, the names count and Count refer to two different variables.
4. C++ keywords can't be used as variable names. A keyword is a word that is part of the C++ language.

Examples for valid variables name:

Variable Name	Legality
Price	Legal
stu_name	Legal
annualprofit	Legal
savings#account	Illegal: Contains the illegal character #
double	Illegal: Is a C++ keyword

3.3 VARIABLE DECLARATION IN C++

Before you can use a variable in a C++ program, it must be declared. A variable declaration tells the compiler the name and datatype of a variable and optionally initializes the variable to a specific value. If you want to use a variable that hasn't been declared, the compiler generates an error message. A variable declaration has the following form:

```
Datatype varname;
```

Datatype specifies the variable type and must be one of the C++ datatype. varname is the variable name, which must follow the rules mentioned earlier. You can declare multiple variables of the same type on one line by separating the variable names with commas:

```
int count, number, start; /* three integer variables */

float percent, total; /* two float variables */
```

3.4 BASIC DATA TYPES IN C++

C++ language has following basic data types:

1. char data type
2. int data type (short and long also)
3. float data type.

3.5 CHAR DATA TYPE

An object of the char data type represents a single character of the character set used by your computer. For example, A is a character, and so is a. But 7 is a number. But a computer can only store numeric code. Therefore, characters such as A, a, B, b, and so on all have a unique numeric code that is used by computers to represent the characters. Usually, a character takes 8 bits (that is, 1 byte) to store its numeric code. You can set the data type of a variable to char by using the following declaration format:

```
char variablename;
or
char variablename1, variablename2, variablename3;
```

Example:

```
char sem,course,colorcode;
```

Character Constants

A character enclosed in single quotes (') is called a character constant. For instance, 'A', 'a', 'B', and 'b' are all character constants that have their unique numeric values in the ASC++II character set.

```
char x = 'a';
char y = 97;
```

PROGRAM 3.1

```
/* Printing out characters */
#include <iostream.h>
void main()
{
    char c1;
    char c2;
    c1 = 'A';
    c2 = 'a';
    cout<<c1;
    cout<<c2;
    }
```

3.6 INT DATA TYPE

The int keyword is used to specify the type of a variable as an integer. Integer numbers are also called whole numbers, which have no fractional part or decimal point. Therefore, the result of an integer division is trunchilded, simply because any fraction part is ignored.

Depending on the operating system and the C++ compiler you're using, the length of an integer varies. On most UNIX/Windows workstations, for example, an integer is 32 bits long, which means that the range of an integer is from 2147483647 to -2147483648. The range of a 16-bit integer at DOS is from 3276732768. Some valid integer values can be 567, 34, 87654, -126 etc.

Declaring Integer Variables

Following shows the basic declaration format:

```
int variablename;
```

Similar to the character declaration, if you have more than one variable to declare, you can use either the format like this:

int variablename1;

int variablename2;

int variablename3;

or like this:

int variablename1, variablename2, variablename3;

PROGRAM 3.2

Printing out numbers on the screen.

```
/* Printing out numbers */
#include <iostraem.h>
void main()
{
int num1
int num2;
cout<<"enter values of num1 and num2";
cin>>num1;
cin>>num2;
cout<<"first number is:"<<num1;
cout<<"second number is:"<<num2;
cout<<"sum of numbers is:"<< num1+num2;
}
```

3.7 FLOAT DATA TYPE

The floating-point number is another data type in the C++ language. Unlike an integer number, a floating-point number contains a decimal point. For instance, 7.01 is a floating-point number; so are 5.71 and -3.14. A floating-point number is also called a real number. A floating-point number is specified by the float keyword in the C++ language.

Like an integer number, a floating-point number has a limited range. The ANSI standard requires that the range be at least plus or minus 1.0*10e37. Normally, a floating-point number is represented by taking 32 bits. Therefore, a floating-point number in C++ is of at least six digits of precision. That is, for a floating-point number, there are at least six digits (or decimal places) on the right side of the decimal point.

Declaring Floating-Point Variables

The following shows the declaration format for a floating-point variable:

```
float variablename;
```

Similar to the character or integer declaration, if you have more than one variable to declare, you can either use the format like this:

```
float variablename1;
float variablename2;
float variablename3;
```

or like the following one:

```
float variablename1, variablename2, variablename3;
```

PROGRAM 3.3

Printing out floating(decimals)numbers on the screen.

```
/* Printing out float numbers */
#include <iostraem.h>
void main()
{
float num1
float num2;
cout<<"enter values of num1 and num2 with decimals like 2.3";
cin>>num1;
cin>>num2;
cout<<"first number is:"<<num1;
cout<<"second number is:"<<num2;
cout<<"sum of numbers is:"<< num1+num2;
}
```

3.8 DOUBLE DATA TYPE

In the C++ language, a floating-point number can also be represented by another data type, called the double data type. In other words, you can specify a variable by the double keyword, and assign the variable a floating-point number.

The difference between a double data type and a float data type is that the former normally uses twice as many bits as the latter. Therefore, a double floating-point number is of at least 10 digits of precision, although the ANSI standard does not specify it for the double data type.

3.9 << AND >> OPERATOR

The symbol << is known as extraction or get from operator, you can use this operator to send some data value on screen, file or in a file. The another symbol >> in known as insertion of put to operator you can use it to read a value from keyboard and put into a variable.

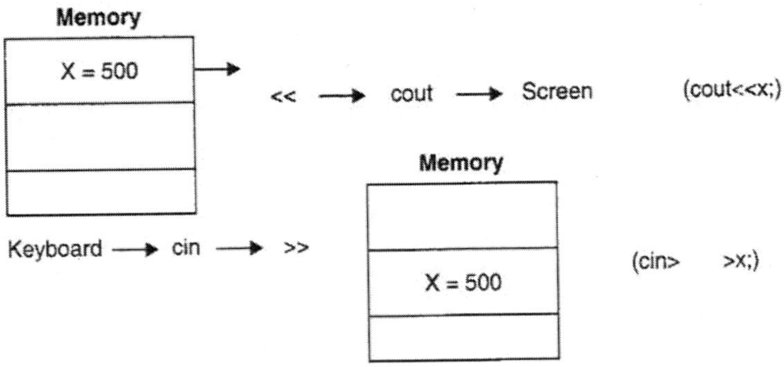

FIGURE 3.1 Use of cin and cout.

3.10 C++ TOKENS

A programmer used C++ tokens to write a C++ program. You can compare it with writing a English sentence there you need noun, verbs, punctuations, symbols to write a proper sentence same is true with a C++ program. You will use C++ tokens to write a program. C++ uses the following types of tokens:

- Identifiers
- Keywords
- Constants
- Operators

3.11 IDENTIFIERS IN C++

An identifier is a user defined name, given to various data items in a program like empname, sturollnumber, bookno etc. If you want to use an identifier in a program use following rules:

1. You can use alphabets(a-z), digits (0-9) and underscore (_) symbol.
2. An identifier cannot start with a number.
3. An identifier cannot start with a _ symbol.
4. sum1 and SUM1 are different identifier because C++ is a case sensitive language.

Some valid identifiers are:

```
number1, net_salary, w123, total, result.
```

Some invalid identifiers are:

```
Bas+salary, 12we, H.rent, hra?rate
```

3.12 C++ KEYWORDS

Some words are reserved by C++, and you may not use them as identifier or variable names. These are keywords used by the C++ compiler to control your program. Followings are the keywords in C++:

auto	break	case	catch
char	class	const	continue
default	delete	do	double
else	enum	extern	float
for	friend	goto	if
int	long	mutable	new
operator	private	protected	public
register	return	short	signed
sizeof	static	struct	switch
template	this	throw	typedef
union	unsigned	virtual	void
volatile	while		

3.13 CONSTANTS AND VARIABLES

A constant is a data storage lochildion, constants don't change their values in a program. You must initialize a constant when you create it, and you cannot assign a new value in future. Like:

```
const pi=3.14, const int rate=25, Const char choice='Y'
```

In C++ a variable is a place in memory to store information. A variable is a lochildion in your computer's memory in which you can store a value and from which you can later retrieve that value. When you define a variable in C++, you must tell the compiler what kind of variable it is: an integer, a character, and so on. This information tells the compiler how much bytes to reserve and what kind of value you want to store in your variable, Because computers use bits and bytes to represent values. Like:

```
int salary, float area, char value etc.

int m1,m2,m3,m4,m5; ( Five integer variables )

float r1,r2,r3,r4; (Four float variables)
```

PROGRAM 3.4

```
#include <iostream.h>
void main()
{
const pi=3.14;
int radius;
float area;
```

```
cout<<"Enter radius of a circle ";
cin>>radius;
area=pi * radius * radius;
cout<<area;
}
```

In above program include, void, main are keywords.Const pi is a constant, int radius, float area are variables , and =, * are operators.

REVIEW QUESTIONS

1. What is the difference between an integar variable and a floating-point variable?
2. What are the differences between an unsigned short int and a long int?
3. What are the advantages of using a symbolic constant rather than a literal constant?
4. What are the advantages of using the const keyword rather than #define?
5. What are rules for a good or bad variable name?
6. Which of the following variable names are good, which are bad, and which are invalid?
   a. Age
   b. !ex
   c. R79J
   d. TotalIncome
   e. _Invalid

LAB EXERCISES

1. What would be the correct variable type in which to store the following information?
   Your age, area of circle, The number of stars in the galaxy, The average rainfall for the month of July in Nainital, To store English alphabets, to store factorial value of 35.
2. Declare variable, store values and display these information using progarm.
3. Declare a constant for pi as 3.14159.
4. Declare a real variable and initialize it using your pi constant.

Chapter 4

STATEMENTS, EXPRESSIONS, AND OPERATORS

4.1 C++ STATEMENT

A statement is a complete direction instructing the computer to carry out some task. In C++, statements are usually written one per line, although some statements can use multiple lines. C++ statements always end with a semicolon (except for preprocessor directives such as #define and #include). Some of C++ statement For examples are:

```
x = 2 + 3;

sum=num1+num2+num3;
```

is an assignment statement. It instructs the computer to add 2 and 3 and to assign the result to the variable x.

4.2 WHITE SPACES

The term white space refers to spaces, tabs, and blank lines in your source code. The C++ compiler isn't sensitive to white space. When the compiler reads a statement in your source code, it looks for the characters in the statement and for the terminating semicolon, but it ignores white space. Thus, the statement

```
x=2+3;
```

is equivalent to this statement:

```
x = 2 + 3;
```

4.3 NULL AND COMPOUND STATEMENTS

Null Statements

If you place a semicolon by itself on a line, you create a null statement—a statement that doesn't perform any action. This is perfectly legal in C++.

Compound Statements

A compound statement, also called a block, is a group of two or more C++ statements enclosed in braces. Here's an example of a block:

```
if (x>3)
{
    cout<<"Hello\n";
    cout<<"world!";
}
```

In C++, a block can be used anywhere a single statement can be used. It's a good idea to place braces on their own lines, making the beginning and end of blocks clearly visible. Placing braces on heir own lines also makes it easier to see whether you've left one out.

4.4 OPERATORS IN C++

An operator is a symbol that instructs C++ to perform some operation, or action, on one or more operands. An operand is something that an operator acts on. In C++, all operands are expressions.

Like c = a + b;

Here + is an operator, while a & b are operands.

C++ offers following operators:

1. The assignment operator
2. Mathematical operators
3. Relational operators
4. Logical operators
5. Address of operator (&)
6. Scope Resolution operator (: :)
7. Bitwise operators

4.4.1 Assignment Operator

The assignment operator is the equal sign (=). Its use in programming is somewhat different from its use in regular math. If you write

```
x = y;
a=560;
```

in a C++ program, it doesn't mean "x is equal to y." Instead, it means "assign the value of y to x." In a C++ assignment statement, the right side can be any expression, and the left side must be a variable name. Thus, the form is as follows:

```
variable = expression;
```

When executed, expression is evaluated, and the resulting value is assigned to variable.

4.4.2 Mathematical Operators

A C++ mathematical operators perform mathematical operations such as addition and subtraction. C++ has two unary mathematical operators (++, - -) and five binary mathematical operators (+, -, *, /, %).

PROGRAM 4.1

```
/* Demo of  unary operators   */
#include <iostream.h>
int a, b;
void  main()

{
/* Set a and b both equal to 5 */
a = b = 5;
/* Print them, decrementing each time. */
/* Use prefix mode for b, postfix mode for a */
cout<< a- - << - -b;
cout<<a - - < - -b;
cout<<- - a<<- -b;
}
```

Use of Binary Operators in C++ Program

PROGRAM 4.2

```
/* Use of  Binary Operators in C++ program */
#include <iostream.h>
void  main()
{
int x;
int y;
int   a,b,c,d,e;
cout<<"enter values of x and y";
cin>>x>>y;
a=x+y;
b=x-y;
```

```
c=x*y;
d=x/y;
e=x%y;
cout<<a;
cout<<b;
cout<<c;
cout<<d;
cout<<e;
}
```

```
if x=50 and y=3  then
a=53
b=47
c=150
d=16
e=2
```

4.4.3 Relational Operators

Ans. C++ relational operators are used to compare expressions, asking questions such as, "Is a greater than 10?" or "Is y equal to 0?" An expression **4.3.3 RELATIONAL OPERATOR** alse (0). C++ has six relational operators:

Operator	Symbol	Example
Equal	==	x == y
Greater than	>	x > y
Less than	<	x < y
Greater than or equal to	>=	x >= y
Less than or equal to	<=	x <= y
Not equal	!=	x!= y

PROGRAM 4.3

```
/* Demo of  relational expressions */
#include <iostream.h>
int x;
void main()
{
x = (7 == 7);                          /* Evaluates to 1 */
cout<<"\n a = (7 = = 7) \n a ="<< x;
x = (7 != 7);                          /* Evaluates to 0 */
```

```
cout<<" \n a = (7 != 7)\n a = "<< x;
x = (12 = = 12) + (7 != 1);            /* Evaluates to 1 + 1 */
cout<<"\na = (12 = = 12) + (7 != 1)\na =\n"<< x;
}
```

4.4.4 Logical Operators

Sometimes you might need to use more than one relational question at once. For example, "If x is Male, have age more than 40 and not a graduate", C++ logical operators allow you to combine two or more relational expressions into a single expression that evaluates to either true or false.

Operator	Symbol	Example
AND	&&	a=5 && b=7
OR	||	x=56 || y=80
NOT	!	!c='s'

4.4.5 Conditional Operators

The conditional operator is C++ only ternary operator, meaning that it takes three operands. Its syntax is:

```
exp1? exp2: exp3;
```

If exp1 evaluates to true (that is, nonzero), the entire expression evaluates to the value of exp2. If exp1 evaluates to false (that is, zero), the entire expression evaluates as the value of exp3. For example, the following statement assigns the value 1 to x if y is true and assigns 100 to x if y is false:

```
x = y? 1: 100;
```

Likewise, to make z equal to the larger of x and y, you could write

```
z = (x > y)? x: y;
```

Perhaps you've noticed that the conditional operator functions somewhat like an if statement. The preceding statement could also be written like this:

```
if (x > y)
z = x;
else
z = y;
```

The conditional operator can't be used in all situations in place of an if...else construction, but the conditional operator is more concise. The conditional operator can also be used in places you can't use an if statement, such as inside a single cout.

Statement:

```
cout<<"The larger value is="<<((x > y)? x: y) );
```

REVIEW QUESTIONS

1. What is an expression?
2. Is x = 15 / 5 an expression? What is its value?
3. What is the value of 201 / 4? (if you will use integer)
4. What is the value of 201 % 4?
5. If myAge, a, and b are all int variables, what are their values after:

```
myAge = 39;
a = myAge++;
b = ++myAge;
```

6. What is the value of 8+2*3?
7. What is the difference between x = 3 and x == 3?
8. Do the following values evaluate to TRUE or FALSE?

   (*a*) 0 (*b*) 1 (*c*) – 1 (*d*) x = 0.

LAB EXERCISES

1. Write a program to add two integer variables and multiply the sum with 13.
2. Examine the following program. While entering three numbers check the output.

```
#include <iostream.h>
int main()
{
 int a, b, c;
cout << "Please enter three numbers\n";
cout << "a: ";
cin >> a;
cout << "\nb: ";
cin >> b;
cout << "\nc: ";
cin >> c;
if (c = (a-b))
{cout << "a: ";
cout << a;
cout << "minus b: ";
cout << b;
cout << "equals c: ";
cout << c << endl;}
else
cout << "a-b does not equal c: " << endl;
return 0;
}
```

3. Enter the program from Exercise 2; compile, link, and run it. Enter the numbers 20, 10, and 50. Did you get the output you expected? Why not?
4. Examine this program and anticipate the output:

```
#include <iostream.h>
void  main()
{
int a = 1, b = 1, c;
if (c = (a-b))
cout << "The value of c is: " << c;
 }
```

5. Enter, compile, link, and run the program from Exercise 4. What will be the output? Why?

Chapter 5

DECISION MAKING IN C++

5.1 DECISION MAKING USING IF

If A student will score 50% marks in each subject he or she will be declared pass in University exam or If your age is 18 years or more you can use your vote to elect your MP or PM. This type of real life situation need conditional programming or decision making, The if statement enables you to test for a condition (such as whether your percentage of marks >50 or not) and branch to different parts of your code, to process other parts.

The simplest form of an if statement is this:

```
if (expression)
 statement;
```

Examples:

```
(A) if(marks>=50)
    {
    char result= 'P' ;
    }
    else
    {
    char result= 'F' ;
    }
```

```
(B) if(Age>=18)
    {
    char vote= 'y';
    }
    else
    {
    char vote= 'n';
    }
```

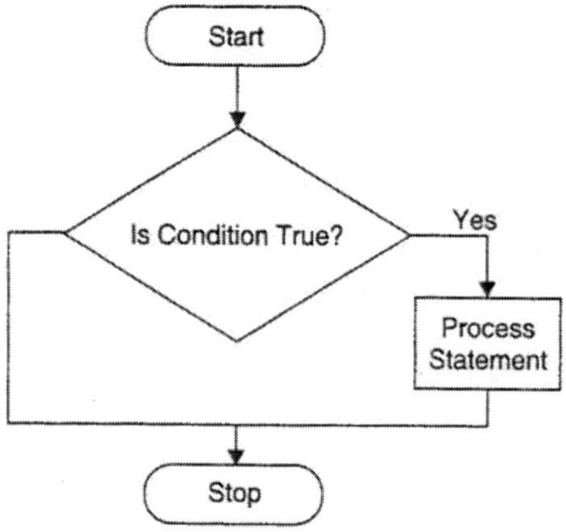

FIGURE 5.1 **Flow chart of If**

You can use multiple statements, as in following example:

```
if (expression)
{
    statement1;
    statement2;
    statement3;
}
if(basic>=8000)
{
da=(basic*67) / 100;
hra=(basic*25) /100
net =basic+da+hra;
}
```

5.2 IF .. ELSE

You can also ask the compiler to check a condition; if that condition is true, the compiler will execute the intended statement. Otherwise, the compiler would execute alternate statement. This is performed using the syntax:

```
if(Condition)
    Statement1;

else
    Statement2;
```

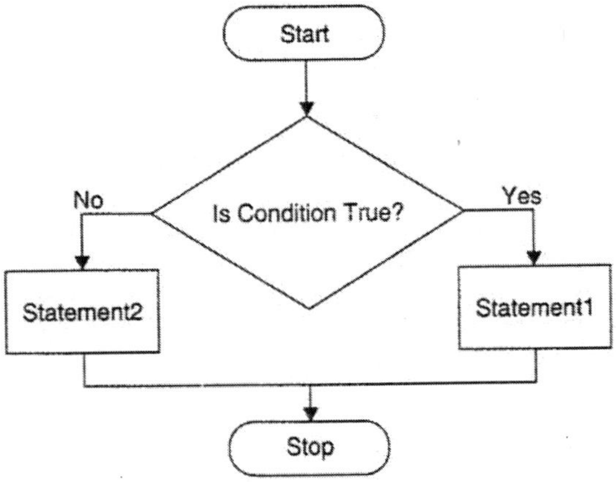

FIGURE 5.2 **Flow chart of nested if**

C++ program to compute netsalary of an employee, netsalary is a sum of basicsalary, da and hra of employee. An employee getting basic salary more than or equal to 8000 will get 67% da, 25% hra on his basic salary otherwise he will get 50% da, 18% hra on his basic salary.

PROGRAM 5.1

```
/* Use of if -else in C++ program */
#include <iostream.h>
void main()
{
int basic ;
float da, hra, netsalary;
cout<<"enter basic salary of employee ";
cin>>basic;
if(basic>=8000)
{
da= basic*67/100;
hra=basic*25/100;
netsalary=basic+da+hra;
}
else
{
 da= basic*50/100;
 hra=basic*18/100;
netsalary=basic+da+hra;
}
cout<<"Netsalary  is"<<netsalary;
}
```

Sometimes, your program will need to check many more than that. The syntax for such a situation is:

```
if(Condition1)
Statement1;

else if(Condition2)
Statement2;
```

An alternative syntax would add the last else as follows:

```
if(Condition1)
    Statement1;

else if(Condition2)
    Statement2;

else if(Condition3)
    Statement3;

else
    Statement-n;
```

The compiler will check the first condition. If Condition1 is true, it will execute Statement1. If Condition1 is false, then the compiler will check the second condition. If Condition2 is true, it will execute Statement2. When the compiler finds a Condition-n to be true, it will execute its corresponding statement. It that Condition-n is false, the compiler will check the subsequent condition. This means you can include as many conditions as you see fit using the else if statement. If after examining all the known possible conditions you still think that there might be an unexpected condition, you can use the optional single else.

PROGRAM 5.2

```
//program to check a character input by keyboard for vowel (a,e,i,o,u)
/* Use of if -else-if in C++ program */
#include <iostream.h>
void main()
{
char alpha;
cout<< " enter a character ";
cin>>alpha;
    if (alpha = = 'a')
{
cout<< "A Vowel ";
}
    else if (alpha = = 'e')
```

```
    {
    cout<< "A Vowel ";
    }
        else if (alpha = = 'i')
        {
        cout<< "A Vowel ";
        }
            else if (alpha = = 'o')
            {
             cout<< "A Vowel ";
            }
                else if (alpha = = 'u')
                {
                cout<< "A Vowel ";
                }
                    else
                    cout<< "Not a Vowel ";
}
```

PROGRAM 5.3

```
#include <iostream.h>
void main()
{
     char Answer;
     cout << "Are you more than 18 (y=Yes/n=No)? ";
     cin >> Answer;
         if( Answer == 'y' )
     {
         cout << "\n You are mature now ";
         cout << "\nYou can vote in election \n";
     }
     else // Any other answer
         cout << "\nWait for more years \n";
 }
```

5.3 MULTIPLE CONDITIONS WITH IF

In many programming problems like result of a students, there can be multiple conditions to allot grade based on percentage of marks secured by the student. In C++ to join multiple conditions you can use && (and) operator or you can use || (or) operator. && is used when both conditions are true while || is used when any one of condition is true. && and || also known as logical operators.

Example:

```
if (temp<=35 && temp >=15)      // both must be true
if(alpha = ='a' || alpha = = 'e' || alpha = = 'i || alpha = = 'o'
                                               || alpha = = 'u')
```

PROGRAM 5.4

```
/* Use of || operator with if -else in C++ program */
#include <iostream.h>
void main()
{
char alpha;
cout<< " enter a character ";
cin>>alpha;
if(alpha = ='a' || alpha = = 'e' || alpha = = 'i || alpha = = 'o' || alpha
= = 'u' )
{
    cout<< "A Vowel ";
    }
else
    {
       cout<< "Not a Vowel ";
}
    }
```

PROGRAM 5.5

```
/* Use of || operator with if -else in C++ program */
#include <iostream.h>
void main()
{
int percentage ;
cout<< "Enter percentage of student (1-100) ";
cin>>percentage;
if ( per <=40)
{
char grade='F';
}
else if ( per>40 && per <=50)
```

```
{
char grade='D';
}
else if ( per>50 && per <=60)
{
char grade='C';
}
else if ( per>60 && per <=70)
{
char grade='B';
}
else
{
char grade='A';
}
cout<< "Grade of student is "<<grade ; }
```

5.4 CONDITIONAL OPERATOR (.:)

In C ++, the conditional operator (?:) can be used in place of if-else statement to check conditions. This is only one operator in C++ which uses three operands. Syntax is

```
Condition? expression1 : expression2
x>y ? 10 : 50
```

PROGRAM 5.6

```
/* Use of ?: in C++ program */
#include <iostream.h>
void main()
{
int x,y ;
cout<< "Enter two numbers ";
cin>>x>>y;
int z = x > y? x : y ;
cout<< "The bigger number is "<< z;
}
```

REVIEW QUESTIONS

1. What is decision making, how it it important in logical design development in a program?
2. Is if (5 + 7 >11) is a valid if statement? What will be the return value of it?
3. What is nested if, describe with the help of an example?
4. What are common operators, used to design multiple conditions in if statement state some examples?
5. If myAge, a, and b are all int variables, what are their values after:

   myAge = 39;

   a = myAge++;

   b = ++myAge;
6. What is the value of 8+2*3?
7. What is the difference between x = 3 and x == 3?
8. Do the following values evaluate to TRUE or FALSE?

   a. 0

   b. 1

   c. -1

   d. x = 0

   e. x == 0 // assume that x has the value of 0

LAB EXERCISES

1. Write a single if statement that examines two integer variables and changes the larger to the smaller, using only one else
   clause.
2. Examine the following program. While entering three numbers, what will be the output?

```
#include <iostream.h>
int main()
{ int a, b, c;
cout << "Please enter three numbers\n";
cout << "a: ";
cin >> a;
cout << "\nb: ";
cin >> b;
cout << "\nc: ";
cin >> c;
if (c = (a-b))
{cout << "a: ";
cout << a;
cout << "minus b: ";
cout << b;
cout << "equals c: ";
cout << c << endl;}
```

```
else
 cout << "a-b does not equal c: " << endl;
 return 0;
 }
```

3. Enter the program from Exercise 2; compile, link, and run it. Enter the numbers 20, 10, and 50. Did you get the output. if yes check.
4. Examine this program and anticipate the output:

```
#include <iostream.h>
int main()
{
int a = 1, b = 1, c;
if (c = (a-b))
cout << "The value of c is: " << c;
return 0;
}
```

5. Write program to check a leap year, input year by keyboard.

Chapter 6

PROGRAM FLOW CONTROLS IN C++

6.1 LOOPS IN C++

Sometimes you want to perform an action again & again, like you want to print first 100 even numbers, then loop concept of C++ will help to do it in less numbers of line of codes. In examination processing system same logic has to repeate for n numbers of students. In a clock seconds, minutes and hours needles make a loop of 60 cycles. Looping, also called iteration, is used in programming to perform the same set of statements over and over until certain specified conditions are met.

Three statements in C++ are designed for looping:

- The for statement
- The while statement
- The do-while statement.

6.2 FOR LOOP

The **for** statement is typically used to count a number of items. At its regular structure, it is divided in three parts. The first section specifies the starting point for the count. The second section sets the counting limit. The last section determines the counting frequency. The syntax of the for statement is:

```
for (expression1; expression2; expression3)
{
 statement1;
 }
```

EXAMPLE 6.1

```
/* Squre & Cube from1 to 15 numbers */
#include <iostream.h>
void main()
{
cout<<"Number"<< "Squre "<<" Cube\n ";
for (int i=1; i<=15; i++)
{
cout<<i<<i*i<<i*i*i;
cout<<"\n";
}
}
```

6.2.1 Multiple Values in a for Loop

EXAMPLE 6.2

```
/* Multiple expressions in for loop */
#include <iostream.h>
void main()
{
    int i, j;
    for (i=0, j=8; i<8; i++, j--)
      cout<<i<<j<<i+j;
}
```

6.2.2 Nested for Loop

A for statement can be executed within another for statement. This is called nesting.By nesting for statements, you can solve complex programming problems.

EXAMPLE 6.3

```
/* Dem of nesting two for statements */
#include <iostream.h>
void mybox( int, int);
void main()
{
      mybox( 5, 25 );
      }
    void mybox( int row, int column )
```

```
        {
           int col;
           for ( ; row > 0; row--)
           {
              for (col = column; col > 0; col--)
        {
              cout<<"*";
        }
        cout<<"\n";
        }
    }
```

6.3 WHILE LOOP

The while statement, also known as while loop, executes a block of statements as long as a specified condition is true. The while statement has the following syntax:

```
while (condition)                 while(x<=10)
{                                 {
statement;                        cout<<x;
statement;                        x=x+2;
increment ;                         }
}
```

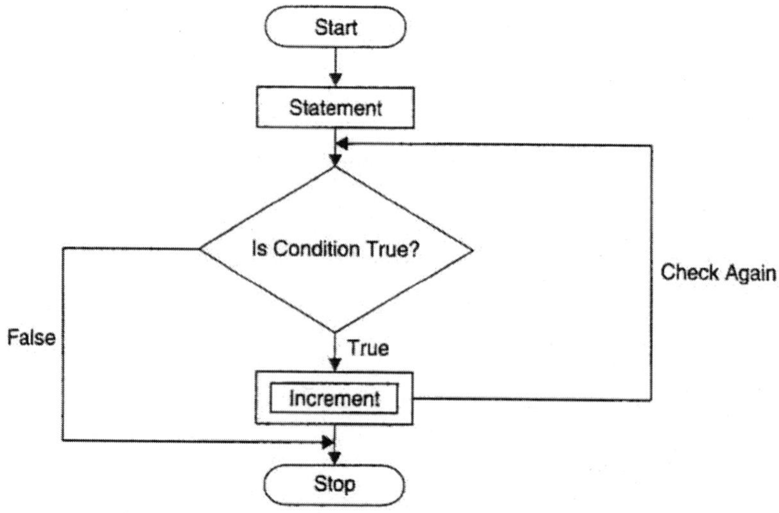

FIGURE 6.1 **while loop**

EXAMPLE 6.4

```
/* Demo of simple while statement */
#include <iostream.h>
int count;
void main()
{
/* Print the numbers 1 through 25 */
count = 1;
while (count <= 25)
    {
    cout<<"Number="<<count;
    count++;
    }
}
```

EXAMPLE 6.5

```
#include <iostream.h>
int number;
void main()
{
int x = 1;
cout<<"enter the number";
cin>>number;
while (x < 10)
{
number=number * x ;
cout<<number<<"\n");
    x++;
}
```

6.4 DO-WHILE LOOP

One more loop in C++ is do...while loop, which executes a block of statements as long as a specified condition is true. The do...while loop tests the condition at the end of the loop rather than at the beginning, as is done by the for loop and the while loop.

The syntax of do...while loop is:

```
do
{
    statement;
    increment / decrement in
loop ;
} while (condition);
```

```
int x=20;
do
{
cout<<x;
x = x - 2;
} while (x > = 2);
```

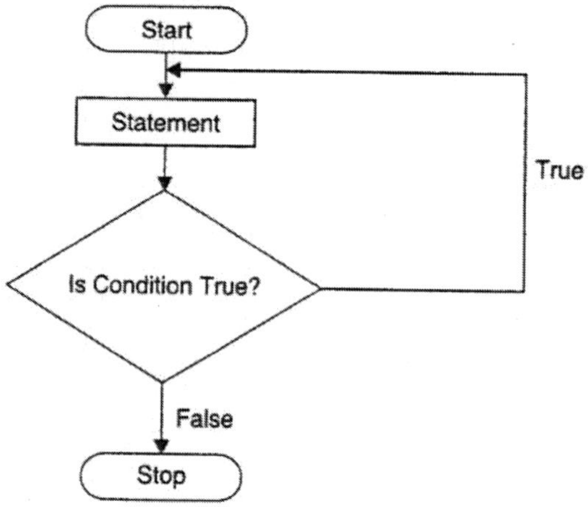

FIGURE 6.2 **do..while loop**

EXAMPLE 6.6

```
/* Demo of do...while statement */
#include <iostream.h
void main()
{
    int selection = 0;
    cout<<"You chose Menu Option \n"<<selection;
    do
    {
        cout<<"\n";
        cout<<"\n1 - Add a Record";
        cout<<"\n2 - Change a record";
        cout<<"\n3 - Delete a record";
        cout<<"\n4 - Quit";
        cout<<"\n" ;
        cout<<"\nEnter a selection: " ;
        cin>>selection ;
    } while ( selection < 1 || selection > 4 );
}
```

6.4.1 The for, the while, or the do...while

If you look at the syntax provided, you can see that any of the three can be used to solve a looping problem. Each has a small twist to what it can do, however. The for statement is best when you know that you need to initialize and increment in your loop. If you only have a condition that you want to meet, and you aren't dealing with a specific number of loops, while is a good choice. If you know that a set of statements needs to be executed at least once, a do...while might be best. Because all three can be used for most problems, the best course is to learn them all and then evaluate each programming situation to determine which is best.

EXAMPLE 6.7

```
#include <iostream.h>
void main()
{
    int sam;
    long lar;
    const int MAX=65535;
    cout << "Enter a small number: ";
    cin >> sam;
    cout << "Enter a large number: ";
    cin >> lar;
    cout << "small: " << sam<< "...";
    while (sam < lar && lar > 0 && sam < MAX)
    {
    if (sam % 5000 = = 0)      // write a * at every 5000 lines
    cout << " * ";
    sam++;
    lar = lar - 2;
    }
    cout << "\nSmall: " << sam << " Large: " << lar << endl;
}
```

6.5 BREAK AND CONTINUE

Any times in a loop if there is a need to return to the top of the loop before the entire set of statements in the loop is executed. The continue statement jumps back to the top of the loop. On the other hand, if you may want to exit the loop before the exit conditions are met. The break statement immediately exits the while loop, and program execution resumes after the closing brace.

```
Loop ( condition )
{
statement1 ;
if ( condition)
    {
continue ;
statement2;
    }
statement3 ;
}
```

```
while (x<=10)
{
cout<<x;
if(x=5)
    {
continue ;
cout<<x+5;
    }
cout<<"end of loop";
}
```

```
Loop ( condition )
{
statement1 ;
if ( condition)
    {
    break ;
statement2;
    }
statement3 ;
    }
```

```
while (x<=10)
{
   cout<<x;
if(x=5)
   {
   break ;
cout<<x+5;
   }
cout<<"end of loop";
```

6.6 INFINITE LOOP

The condition you use for testing in a while loop can be any valid C++ expression. As long as that condition remains true, the while loop will continue. You can create a infinite loop that will never end by using the number 1 for the condition to be tested. Since 1 is always true, the loop will never end, unless a break statement is reached. like:

EXAMPLE 6.8

```
#include <iostream.h>
void main()
{
    int counter = 0;
       while (1) //infinite loop
       {
          counter ++;
          if (counter > 25)
          break;          //break condition
       }
       cout << "Counter: " << counter << "\n";
}
```

Output: Counter: 26

6.7 WHILE Vs DO .. WHILE LOOP

It is possible that the body of a while loop will never execute. The while statement checks its condition *before* executing any of its statements, and if the condition evaluates false, the entire body of the while loop is skipped. The do...while loop executes the body of the loop before its condition is tested and ensures that the body always executes at least one time.

EXAMPLE 6.9

```
// Demonstrates do while
#include <iostream.h>
void main()
{
    int counter;
    cout << "How many hellos in loop you want? ";
    cin >> counter;
    do
    {
       cout << "Hello Friend \n";
       counter--;
    } while (counter >0 );
    cout << "Value of Counter is: " << counter << endl;
}
```

Output: How many hellos in loop you want? 2
Hello
Hello
Value of Counter is: 0

In above program the user is prompted for enter a starting value, which is stored in the integer variable counter. In the do...while loop, the body of the loop is entered before the condition is tested, and therefore the body of the loop is guaranteed to run at least once even the condition can be false.

6.8 SWITCH STATEMENT

For decision making based programs, you have seen the use of if and if/else statements. These can become quite confusing when if nested too deeply, but in C++ we have an alternative. Use switch statement, unlike if, which evaluates one value, switch statements allow you to branch on any of a number of different values. The general form of the switch statement is:

```
switch (condition / expression )
{
case One: statement;
          break;
case Two: statement;
          break;
case N:   statement;
          break;
default:  statement;
}
```

EXAMPLE 6.10

```
// Demonstrates switch statement
#include <iostream.h>
void main()
{
    int number;
    cout << "Enter a number between 1 and 7: ";
    cin >> number;
    switch (number)
    {
    case 0: cout << "Amrapali Institute, Haldwani -List of courses!";
       break;
    case 6: cout << "B.Tech!\n";
    case 5: cout << "MCA!\n";
    case 4: cout << "MBA!\n";
    case 3: cout << "BBA!\n";
    case 2: cout << "BCA!\n";
    case 1: cout << "BHMCT!\n";
       break;
    default: cout << "Please enter value 1-6!\n";
       break;
    }
    cout << "\n\n";
}
```

Output: Enter a number between 1 and 6: 3

BBA!

BCA!

BHMCT!

Enter a number between 1 and 6: 8

Please enter value 1-5!

REVIEW QUESTIONS

1. How do you initialize more than one variable in a for loop?
2. Why is go to avoided?
3. Is it possible to write a for loop with a body that is never executed?
4. Is it possible to nest while loops within for loops?
5. Is it possible to create a loop that never ends? Give an example.
6. What happens if you create a loop that never ends?

LAB EXERCISES

1. What is the value of x when the for loop completes?

```
for (int x = 0; x < 100; x++)
```

2. Write a nested for loop that prints a table upto 10.
3. Write a for statement to count from 100 to 200 by 2s.
4. Write a while loop to count from 100 to 200 by 2s.
5. Write a do...while loop to count from 100 to 200 by 2s.
6. Find error: What is wrong with this code?

```
int counter = 0
while (counter < 10)
{
        cout << "counter: " << counter;
}
```

7. Find error: What is wrong with this code?

```
for (int counter = 0; counter < 10; counter++);
        cout << counter << " ";
```

8. Find error: What is wrong with this code?

```
int counter = 100;
while (counter < 10)
{
        cout << "counter now: " << counter;
        counter—;
}
```

9. Find error: What is wrong with this code?

```
cout << "Enter a number between 0 and 5: ";
cin >> theNumber;
switch (theNumber)
{
        case 0:
                doZero();
        case 1: // fall through
        case 2: // fall through
        case 3: // fall through
        case 4: // fall through
        case 5:
                doOneToFive();
                break;
        default:
                doDefault();
                break;
}
```

Chapter 7

FUNCTIONS IN C++

7.1 FUNCTION

A function is a block of statements with a name. In your mobile set you have several functions like call a number, send a SMS or read a message. Any time you can use that without defining that, this is true with C++ functions. Once a function has been designed you can call it to perform your task. Each function has a unique name. By using that name in another part of the program, you can execute the statements contained in the function. This is known as calling the function. A function can be called from within another function. A function is independent. A function can perform its task without interference from or interfering with other parts of the program. A function performs a specific task like send your photo to your girl friend using MMS services of your handset. This is the easy part of the definition. A task is a discrete job that your program must perform as part of its overall operation, such as sending a line of text to a printer, sorting an array into numerical order, or calculating a cube root. A function can return a value to the calling program like your messege has been delivered. When your program calls a function, the statements it contains are executed. If you want them to, these statements can pass information back to the calling program.

7.2 FUNCTIONAL PROGRAMMING

If you want to work with functions in C++, you should use the following steps:

(*a*) **prototype the function**

```
//int sum ( int, int )
```

(*b*) **define the function**

```
 //int sum( int x, int y )
{
z = x + y ;
return z ;
}
```

(*c*) **use or call the functions**

```
// z=sum(a,b);
```

EXAMPLE 7.1

```
/* Demo of function for sum */
#include <iostream.h>
int sum(int, int ); // function prototype
int x, y, z ;
void main()
{
    cout<<"Enter two numbers: ";
    cin>>x>>y;
    z = sum (x, y); //function call
    cout<<"The Sum of numbers is\n"<<z;
}
// function definition
int sum (int x, int y )
{
    return x+y;
}
```

EXAMPLE 7.2

```
/* Demo of function for cube */
#include <stdio.h>
long cube(long x);
long input, answer;
void main()
{
    cout<<"Enter an integer value: ";
    cin>>input;
    answer = cube(input);
    cout<<"The cube of number is\n"<<input<<answer;
}
```

```
/* Function: cube() - calculates the cubed value of a variable */
long cube(long x)
{
     long x_cubed;
     x_cubed = x * x * x;
     return x_cubed;
}
```

7.3 FUNCTION PROTOTYPE Vs DEFINITION

A function prototype provides the compiler with a description of a function that will be defined at a later point in the program. The prototype includes a return type indichilding the type of variable that the function will return. It also includes the function name, which should describe what the function does. The prototype also contains the variable types of the arguments that will be passed to the function. Optionally, it can contain the names of the variables that will be passed. A prototype should always end with a semicolon.

Like:

```
return_type function_name( arg-type name-1,...,arg-type name-n);
int squre (int x);
double amount(int p, float r, int time);
```

A function definition is the actual function. The definition contains the code that will be executed. The first line of a function definition, called the function header, should be identical to the function prototype, with the exception of the semicolon. A function header shouldn't end with a semicolon. In addition, although the argument variable names were optional in the prototype, they must be included in the function header. Following the header is the function body, containing the statements that the function will perform. The function body should start with an opening bracket and end with a closing bracket. If the function return type is anything other than void, a return statement should be included, returning a value matching the return type.

Like:

```
returntype functionname( argtype name1,...,argtype name n)
{
     /* statements; */
}
int squre (int x)
{
int sq;
sq= x * x * x;
return sq;
}
```

EXAMPLE 7.3

```
#include <iostream.h>
int x, y, z;
int larger( int, int );
void main()
{
    cout<<"Enter two different integer values: ";
    cin>>x>>y;
    z = larger( x, y);
    cout<<"\n The larger value is "<<z;
}
int larger( int a, int b)
{
    if (a > b)
    return a;
    else
    return b;
}
```

EXAMPLE 7.4

```
// tempeture conversion function
#include <iostream.h>
float Convert(float);
void main()
{
    float TempFer;
    float TempCel;
    cout << "Please enter the temperature in Fahrenheit: ";
    cin >> TempFer;
    TempCel = Convert(TempFer);
    cout << "\nHere's the temperature in Celsius: ";
    cout << TempCel << endl;
}
float Convert(float TempFer)
{
    float TempCel;
    TempCel = ((TempFer - 32) * 5) / 9;
    return TempCel;
}
```

EXAMPLE 7.5

```
//function to differentiate local and global variables in a program.
#include <iostream.h>
void myFunction(); // function prototype
int x = 50, y = 70; // declare global variables
void main()
{
    cout << "x from main: " << x << "\n";
    cout << "y from main: " << y << "\n\n";
    myfunction();
       cout << "Back from myfunction!\n\n";
       cout << "x from main: " << x << "\n";
       cout << "y from main: " << y << "\n";
}
void myfunction()
{
    int y = 100; //declare local variable
    cout << "x from myfunction: " << x << "\n";
    cout << "y from myfunction: " << y << "\n\n";
}
```

EXAMPLE 7.6

```
// showing variables scope within a block
#include <iostream.h>
void myfunc();
void main()
{
int x = 55;
cout << "\nIn main x is: " << x;
myfunc(); //calling the function
cout << "\nBack in main, x is: " << x;
}
void myfunc()
{
int x =88;
cout << "\n In myfunc, local x: " << x << endl;
    {
    cout << "\nIn block in myfunc, x is: " << x;
    int x =99;
```

```
    cout << "\nVery local x: " << x;
    }
cout << "\nOut of block, in myfunc, x: " << x << endl;
}
```

EXAMPLE 7.7

```
// function to interchange / swap two numbers
#include <iostream.h>
void swap(int x, int y);
void main()
{
int x = 25, y = 110;
cout << "Main. Before swap, x: " << x << " y: " << y << "\n";
swap(x,y);
cout << "Main. After swap, x: " << x << " y: " << y << "\n";
}
void swap (int x, int y)
{
    int temp;
    cout << "Swap. Before swap, x: " << x << " y: " << y << "\n";
    temp = x;
    x = y;
    y = temp;
    cout << "Swap. After swap, x: " << x << " y: " << y << "\n";
}
```

7.4 RETURN MULTIPLE VALUES BY FUNCTION

A function must return a value to calling function or it should return void. Void is a signal to the compiler that no value will be returned. To return a value from a function, you should use the keyword return followed by the value you want to return. For example:

```
return x;
return a*b*c;
```

This is a single return value but a function can return multiple values to calling function like given example:

EXAMPLE 7.8

```
// demo of multiple return statements
#include <iostream.h>
```

```
int double(int amounttodouble);
void main()
{
    int result = 0;
    int input;
    cout << "Enter a number between 0 and 5000 to double: ";
    cin >> input;
    cout << "\n Before double is called... ";
    cout << "\ninput: " << input << " doubled: " << result << "\n";
    result = double(input);
    cout << "\nBack from double...\n";
    cout << "\ninput: " << input << " doubled: " << result << "\n";
}
    int double(int original)
    {
        if (original <= 5000)
            return original * 2;
        else
            return -1;
        cout << "You can't enter >5000 \n";
    }
```

7.5 RECURSION

The term recursion refers to a situation in which a function calls itself either directly or indirectly. Indirect recursion occurs when one function calls another function that then calls the first function. C++ allows recursive functions, and they can be useful in some situations.

For example, recursion can be used to calculate the factorial of a number. The factorial of a number x is written x! and is calculated as follows:

```
x! = x * (x-1) * (x-2) * (x-3) * ... * (2) * 1
```

However, you can also calculate x! like this:

```
x! = x * (x-1)!
```

EXAMPLE 7.9

```
// Demo of recursion. To calculates the factorial of a number.
#include <iostraem.h>
unsigned int f, x;
unsigned int factorial(unsigned int a);
void main()
```

```
{
cout<<"Enter an integer value between 1 and 8: ";
cin>>x;
if( x > 8 || x < 1)
{
    cout<<"Only values from 1 to 8 are acceptable!";
}
else
{
    f = factorial(x);
    cout<<" factorial equals"<<f);
}
  }
unsigned int factorial(unsigned int a)
{
    if (a = = 1)
    return 1;
    else
    {
    a = a * factorial(a-1);
    return a;
    }
}
```

EXAMPLE 7.10

```
// program to print Fibonacci numbers
// Uses this algorithm: Fib(n) = fib(n-1) + fib(n-2)
#include <iostream.h>
void fib(int n);
void main()
{
    int n, answer;
    cout << "Enter number to find: ";
    cin >> n;
    cout << "\n\n";

    answer = fib(n);
    cout << answer << " is the " << n << "th Fibonacci number\n";
    }
```

```
    int fib (int n)
    {
    cout << "Processing fib(" << n << ")... ";
    if (n < 3 )
    {
    cout << "Return 1!\n";
    return (1);
    }
    else
    {
    cout << "Call fib(" << n-2 << ") and fib(" << n-1 << ").\n";
    return( fib(n-2) + fib(n-1));
    }
}
```

7.6 FUNCTION OVERLOADING

In C++ you can define more than one function with the same name. This is known as function overloading. The functions must differ in their parameter list, with a different type of parameter, a different number of parameters, or both.

Like:

```
int sum (int, int);              // two add two integer numbers
int sum (long, long);            // two add two long numbers
int sum (float, float, float); // two add two float
```

sum() is overloaded with three different parameter lists. The return types can be the same or different on overloaded functions. If you will use two functions with the same name and parameter list, but different return types, they will generate a compiler error.

Function overloading is also known as function polymorphism a feature of object oriented programming. Poly means many, and morph means form: a polymorphic function is many-formed.

EXAMPLE 7.11

```
// demonstrates of function overloading / polymorphism
#include <iostream.h>
int Double(int);
long Double(long);
float Double(float);
double Double(double);
void main()
```

```
{
    int myInt = 6500;
    long myLong = 65000;
    float myFloat = 6.5F;
    double myDouble = 6.5e20;
    int doubledInt;
    long doubledLong;
    float doubledFloat;
    double doubledDouble;
    cout << "myInt: " << myInt << "\n";
    cout << "myLong: " << myLong << "\n";
    cout << "myFloat: " << myFloat << "\n";
    cout << "myDouble: " << myDouble << "\n";
    doubledInt = Double(myInt);
    doubledLong = Double(myLong);
    doubledFloat = Double(myFloat);
    doubledDouble = Double(myDouble);
    cout << "doubledInt: " << doubledInt << "\n";
    cout << "doubledLong: " << doubledLong << "\n";
    cout << "doubledFloat: " << doubledFloat << "\n";
    cout << "doubledDouble: " << doubledDouble << "\n";
    }
    int Double(int original)
    {
    cout << "In Double(int)\n";
    return 2 * original;
    }
    long Double(long original)
    {
    cout << "In Double(long)\n";
    return 2 * original;
    }
    float Double(float original)
    {
    cout << "In Double(float)\n";
    return 2 * original;
    }
    double Double(double original)
    {
    cout << "In Double(double)\n";
    return 2 * original;
  }
```

REVIEW QUESTIONS

1. What is functional programming?
2. Write about function prototype in C++.
3. Differintiate between function overloading and function overriding with examples.
4. Write few examples of recursion in computer programming.
5. How can you return or pass objects in a function.

LAB EXERCISES

1. Write a program to use the given function:

```
void SquareArea()
{
        double Side;
        cout << "\nEnter the side of the square: ";
        cin >> Side;
        cout << "\nSquare characteristics:";
        cout << "\nSide = " << Side;
        cout << "\nArea = " << Side * Side;
}
```

2. Write a function swap() to swap the values of two float, int, long numbers.
3. Design a function to convert decimal number into binary number.
4. Design a function plandrome() to check a number and string, is it plandrome.

Chapter 8

FUNDAMENTALS OF CLASSES AND OBJECTS

8.1 CLASSES

Programs are usually written to solve real-world problems, such as keeping track of employee records in an organization like Amrapali Institute or simulating the workings of a heating system. Although it is possible to solve complex problems by using programs written with only integers and characters data types, but it is more easier to solve large, complex problems if you can create objects using base classes. In other words, simulating the workings of a heating system is easier if you can create variables that represent rooms, heat sensors, thermostats, and boilers. The closer these variables correspond to reality, the easier it is to write the program. To solve real world problems there is a need to create new data types also known as user defined data types, a class help us to design a new data type with attributes and operations or functions in a single unit. A class defines a data type, much like a struct C. In a computer science sense, a type consists of both a set of states and a set of operations which transition between those states. You can make a new data type by declaring a class. A class is just a collection of variables often of different types combined with a set of related functions. One way to think about a car is as a collection of wheels, doors, seats, windows, and so forth. Another way is to think about what a car can do: It can move, speed up, slow down, stop, park, and so on. A class enables you to encapsulate, or bundle, these various parts and various functions into one collection, which is called an object.

CAR class
wheels
doors
seats
windows
Functions
Move
Start
Stop
Park

FIGURE 8.1 a CAR class

```
CAR c1,c2;
```

Two Objects of CAR, having same Attributes and Functions

Encapsulating everything you know about a car into one class has a number of advantages for a programmer. Everything is now in one place, which makes it easy to refer to, copy, and manipulate the data using objects of class.

8.2 OBJECTS

In Object oriented programming languages like C++, "object" usually means "an instance of a class." Thus a class defines the behavior of possibly many objects.You can say now an object is an individual instance of a class. You can define an object of your new class just as you define an integer variable. Like:

```
Car c1, // One object of Car class

Employee e1,e2, //Two objects of Employee class

Student s1,s2,s3 // Three objects of student class
```

CAR class
wheels
doors
seats
windows
Functions
Move
Start
Stop
Park

CAR	c1;
Class	Object
Wheels	Move
Doors	Start
Seats	Stop
Windows	Park
Data members	Functions

EXAMPLE 8.1

a class employee with following attributes empno, empname,empdept, empsalary and functions join, computesalary, printdata, printsalary.

Class employee
Empno - integer
Empname - string
Empdent - string
Empsalary - integer
Functions
Join()
Computesalary()
Printdata()
Printsalary()

EXAMPLE 8.2

a class bankaccount with following attributes accno, custname, custadd, openamount, closingamount and functions open, deposit, withdrawal, checkbalance, close.

Class bankaccount
Accno - integer
Custname - string
Custadd - string
Openamount - integer
Closingamount - integer
Functions
Open()
Deposit()
Withdrawl()
Checkbalance()
Close()

8.3 MEMBER VARIABLES AND MEMBER FUNCTIONS

A class can consist of any combination of the variable types and also other class types. The variables in the class are referred to as the member variables or data members. Like a Car class might have member variables representing the seats, windows, doors, tires etc. Member variables, also known as data members, are the variables in your class. Member variables are part of your class, just like the wheels and engine are part of your car class. The functions in the class typically manipulate the member variables. They are referred to as member functions or methods of the class. Methods of the Car class might include Start() and Stop(). Member functions, also known as methods, are the functions in your class. Member functions are as much a part of your class as the member variables. They determine what the objects of your class can do.

8.4 CLASS DECLARATION

To declare a class, use the class keyword followed by an opening brace, and then list the data members and methods of that class. End the declaration with a closing brace and a semicolon. Here's the declaration of a class called Car:

```
class Car
{
int doors; //member variable
int wheels;
Start(); //member function
Stop();
};
```

Declaring this class doesn't allocate memory for a Car. It just tells the compiler what a Car is, what data it contains (wheels and doors), and what it can Start() and Stop(). It also tells the compiler the size of a Car in bytes, to know how much bytes the compiler must set aside for each Car object that you will create in future. In this example, if an integer is two bytes, a Car is only four bytes big: doors is two bytes, and wheels is another two bytes. Start() and Stop() takes up no bytes, because no storage space is reserved for member functions.

8.5 PUBLIC Vs PRIVATE

Some more keywords are used in the declaration of a class. Two of the most important are public and private. All members of a class data and methods are private by default. Private members can be accessed only within methods of the class itself. Public members can be accessed through any object of the class. This distinction is both important and confusing. To make it a bit clearer, consider an example from earlier in this chapter:

```
class Car
{
int doors;
int wheels;
Start();
Stop();
};
```

In this declaration, doors, wheels, Start() and Stop() are all private, because all members of a class are private by default. This means that unless you specify otherwise, they are private. However, if you now declare object of Car class like:

```
Car c1;
c1.wheels=6; // error! can't access private data!
```

the compiler will show this as an error. Because you can not access private data values directly.

Now change the class declaration as:

```
class Car
{
public:
int doors;
int wheels;
Start();
Stop();
};
```

EXAMPLE 8.3

```
#include <iostream.h>
class Car                    // declare the class object
{
public:                      // members which follow are public
    int wheels;
    int doors;
};
void main()
{
    Car maruti; //Object declaration
    maruti.wheels = 4; // assign to the member variable
    cout << "Maruti is a car which has " ;
    cout << maruti.wheels << " Wheels\n";
}
```

EXAMPLE 8.4

```
//add and subtract two numbers using classes and objects
#include <iostream.h>
class addsub
{
int x;
int y; //private data members
```

```
public:
void twosum();                  //public member function
void twosub();
};                              // class defined
    void addsub::twosum()       //define member function
{
cin>>x;
cin>>y;
int z=x+y;
cout<< "Sum is ="<<z;
}

void addsub::twosub()
{
cin>>x;
cin>>y;
int z=x-y;
cout<< "Subtraction is ="<<z;
}
void main()
{
addsub s;         //object declaration of addsub class
s.twosum();       // calling member function with object
s.twosub();
}
```

EXAMPLE 8.5

```
//multiply and divide two numbers using classes and objects
#include <iostream.h>
class addsub
{
int x;
int y;                  //private data members
public:
void twomult()          //public member function inside class
{
cin>>x;
cin>>y;
int z=x*y;
cout<< "Product is ="<<z;
}
```

```
void twodiv()
{
cin>>x;
cin>>y;
int z=x-y;
cout<< "Division is ="<<z;
}
};      // class defined


void main()
{
addsub s;          //object declaration of addsub class
s.twomult();       // calling member function with object
s.twodiv();
}
```

8.6 CONSTRUCTOR AND DESTRUCTORS

If you define an integer and immediately initialize it in a C++ program like:

```
int length = 7; // define and initialize to 7
```

Initialization combines the definition of the variable with its initial assignment. You have freedom to change that value later in program. Initialization ensures that your variable is never without a meaningful value say garbage.

How do you initialize the member data of a class? Classes have a special member function called a constructor. The constructor can take parameters as needed, but it cannot have a return value not even void. The constructor in a class must have the same name as the class itself, so if you have car class the name of constructor will be car.

Whenever you declare a constructor, you'll also want to declare a destructor. Just as constructors create and initialize objects of your class, destructors clean up after your object and free any memory you might have allochilded. A destructor always has the name of the class, preceded by a tilde (~). Destructors take no arguments and have no return value. Therefore, the car declaration includes ~car();

8.7 TYPES OF CONSTRUCTORS

If you don't declare a constructor or a destructor, the compiler makes one for you. Known as default constructor and destructor, it takes no arguments and do nothing. You can declare an object without passing in parameters, such as:

```
Car c1; // c1 gets no parameters
```

you must have a constructor in the form:

```
Car();
```

When you define an object of a class, the constructor is called. If the Car constructor took two parameters, you might define a Car object by writing:

```
Car c1(5,7);
```

If the constructor took one parameter, you would write

```
Car c1(3);
```

In the event that the constructor takes no parameters at all, you leave off the parentheses and write

```
Car c1 ;
```

This is an exception to the rule that states all functions require parentheses, even if they take no parameters. This is why you are able to write

```
Car c1;
```

which is a call to the default constructor. It provides no parameters, and it leaves off the parentheses. You don't have to use the compiler-provided default constructor. You are always free to write your own constructor with no parameters. Even constructors with no parameters can have a function body in which they initialize their objects or do other work. As a matter of form, if you declare a constructor, be sure to declare a destructor, even if your destructor does nothing. Although it is true that the default destructor would work correctly, it doesn't hurt to declare your own. It makes your code clearer.

EXAMPLE 8.6

```
// Demo of declaration of a constructors and
// destructor for the child class
#include <iostream.h>        // for cout
class child                  // begin declaration of the class
{
public:                      // begin public section
child(int initialAge);       // constructor
~child();                    // destructor
int GetAge();                // accessor function
void SetAge(int age);        // accessor function
void cry();
private:                     // begin private section
int itsAge;                  // member variable
};
```

```
// constructor of child
child::child(int initialAge)
{
itsAge = initialAge;
}
child::~child()      // destructor, takes no action
{
}

// GetAge, Public accessor function
// returns value of itsAge member
int child::GetAge()
{
return itsAge;
}

// Definition of SetAge, public
// accessor function
void child::SetAge(int age)
{

// set member variable its age to
// value passed in by parameter age
itsAge = age;
}

// definition of cry method
// returns: void
// parameters: None
// action: Prints "cry" to screen
void child::cry()
{
cout << "Cry\n";
}

// create a child, set its age, have it
// cry, tell us its age, then cry again.
void main()
```

```
{
child vama(4);
vama.cry();
cout << "Vama is a child who is " ;
cout << vama.GetAge() << " years old.\n";
vama.cry();
vama.SetAge(7);
cout << "Now Vama is " ;
cout << vama.GetAge() << " years old.\n";
}
```

8.8 CONSTRUCTOR OVERLOADING

Constructors, like all member functions, can be overloaded. The ability to overload constructors is very powerful and very flexible. For example, we can design a rectangle class that has two constructors: The first takes a length and a width and makes a rectangle of that size. The second takes no values and makes a default-sized rectangle as shown in example.

EXAMPLE 8.7

```
// Overloading constructors
#include <iostream.h>
class Rectangle
{
public:
Rectangle();
Rectangle(int width, int length);
~Rectangle() {}
int GetWidth() const { return itsWidth; }
int GetLength() const { return itsLength; }
private:
int itsWidth;
int itsLength;
};
Rectangle::Rectangle()
{
    itsWidth = 5;
    itsLength = 10;
}
```

```
Rectangle::Rectangle (int width, int length)
{
    itsWidth = width;
    itsLength = length;
}
void main()
{
    Rectangle Rect1;
    cout << "Rect1 width: " << Rect1.GetWidth() << endl;
    cout << "Rect1 length: " << Rect1.GetLength() << endl;
    int aWidth, aLength;
    cout << "Enter a width: ";
    cin >> aWidth;
    cout << "\nEnter a length: ";
    cin >> aLength;
    Rectangle Rect2(aWidth, aLength);
    cout << "\nRect2 width: " << Rect2.GetWidth() << endl;
    cout << "Rect2 length: " << Rect2.GetLength() << endl;
}
```

8.9 "new" AND "delete" KEYWORDS

Use of new

To allocate memory for objects or variables you can use the new keyword. new is followed by the type of the object that you want to allocate so that the compiler knows how much memory is required. Therefore, new unsigned short int allocates two bytes in the free store, and new long allocates four bytes.

The return value from new is a memory address. It must be assigned to a pointer. To create an unsigned short on the free store, you might write

```
unsigned short int * myp;
myp = new unsigned short int;
```

You can, of course, initialize the pointer at its creation with

```
unsigned short int * myp = new unsigned short int;
```

In either case, myp now points to an unsigned short int on the free store. You can use this like any other pointer to a variable and assign a value into that area of memory by writing

```
*myp = 56;
```

This means, "allocate 56 at the value in myp," or "Assign the value 56 to the area on the free store to which myp points."

If new cannot create memory on the free store (memory is, after all, a limited resource) it returns the null pointer. You must check your pointer for null each time you request new memory.

Use of delete

When you are finished with your area of memory, you must call delete on the pointer. delete returns the memory to the free store. Remember that the pointer itself—as opposed to the memory to which it points—is a local variable. When the function in which it is declared returns, that pointer goes out of scope and is lost. The memory allocated with new is not freed automatically, however. That memory becomes unavailable—a situation called a memory leak. It's called a memory leak because that memory can't be recovered until the program ends. It is as though the memory has leaked out of your computer. To restore the memory to the free store, you use the keyword delete. For example,

```
delete myp;
```

EXAMPLE 8.8

```
//Creating and deleting objects using new and delete.

#include <iostream.h>
class mycat
{
public:
    mycat();
    ~mycat();
private:
    int Age;
};
mycat::mycat()
{
    cout << "Constructor called.\n";
    Age = 1;
}
mycat::~mycat()
{
    cout << "Destructor called.\n";
}
void main()
{
    cout << "mycat juli \n";
    mycat juli;
```

```
        cout << "mycat *pcat = new mycat \n";
        mycat * pcat = new mycat;
        cout << "delete pcat.\n";
        delete pcat ;
        cout << "check where is juli \n";
    }
```

8.10 "THIS" POINTER

Every class member function has a hidden parameter: the this pointer. this points to the individual object. The this pointer point to the object used to invoke a member function. All class methods have a this pointer set to the address of a object invoking the method. like:

```
emp e1;
e1.setdata();
```

now this pointer will set for the address of e1 object.

```
emp e2;
e2.setdata();
```

now this pointer will set for the address of e2 object

REVIEW QUESTIONS

1. What is the dot operator, and what is it used for?
2. Which sets aside memory—declaration or definition?
3. Is the declaration of a class its interface or its implementation?
4. What is the difference between public and private data members?
5. Can member functions be private?
6. Can member data be public?
7. If you declare two Cat objects, can they have different values in their itsAge member data?
8. Do class declarations end with a semicolon? Do class method definitions?
9. What would the header for a Cat function, Meow, that takes no parameters and returns void look like?
10. What function is called to initialize a class?

LAB EXERCISES

1. Write the code that declares a class called Employee with these data members: age, yearsOfService, and Salary.

2. Rewrite the Employee class to make the data members private, and provide public accessor methods to get and set each of the data members.
3. Write a program with the Employee class that makes two Employees; sets their age, YearsOfService, and Salary; and prints their values.
4. Continuing from Exercise 3, provide a method of Employee that reports how many thousands of dollars the employee earns, rounded to the nearest 1,000.
5. Change the Employee class so that you can initialize age, YearsOfService, and Salary when you create the employee.
6. What is wrong with the following declaration?

```
class Square
{
public:
 int Side;
}
```

7. Why isn't the following class declaration very useful?

```
class Cat
{
        int GetAge()const;
private:
        int itsAge;
};
```

8. What three bugs in this code will the compiler find?

```
class TV
{
public:
        void SetStation(int Station);
        int GetStation() const;
private:
        int itsStation;
};
main()
{
        TV myTV;
        myTV.itsStation = 9;
        TV.SetStation(10);
        TV myOtherTv(2);
}
```

Chapter 9

ARRAYS AND POINTERS

9.1 ARRAY OF OBJECTS

Any object, whether built-in or user-defined, can be stored in an array. When you declare the array, you tell the compiler the type of object to store and the number of objects for which to allocate room. The compiler knows how much room is needed for each object based on the class declaration. The class must have a default constructor that takes no arguments so that the objects can be created when the array is defined.

FIGURE 9.1 **an array of faces**

S	A	C	H	I	N	T	E	N	D	U	L	K	A	R

FIGURE 9.2 **an array of characters**

An array is a clooection of similer data values in a single unit.

Accessing member data in an array of objects is a two-step process. You identify the member of the array by using the index operator ([ ]), and then you add the member operator (.) to access the particular member variable. Like:

- int x[10];   //array of 10 integer data types
- float y[12];   //array of 12 float data types
- child c[5];   // array of 5 child class objects.

EXAMPLE 9.1

```
// Demo - An array of objects
#include <iostream.h>
class CHILD
{
    public:
       CHILD() { itsAge = 1; itsWeight=5; }
       ~CHILD() {}
       int GetAge() const { return itsAge; }
       int GetWeight() const { return itsWeight; }
       void SetAge(int age) { itsAge = age; }
       private:
       int itsAge;
       int itsWeight;
};
void main()
{
    CHILD suhani[5]; // array of objects of CHILD class
    int i;
    for (i = 0; i < 5; i++)
       suhani[i].SetAge(2*i +1);
    for (i = 0; i < 5; i++)
    {
    cout << "Child #" << i+1<< ": ";
    cout << suhani[i].GetAge() << endl;
    }
}
```

9.2 ARRAY OF POINTERS

The arrays of objects usually store all their members in a stack. Usually stack memory is severely limited, whereas free store memory is far larger. It is possible to declare each object on the free store and then to store only a pointer to the object in the array. This dramatically reduces the amount of stack memory used and fasten the processing speed. As an indiaimcaion of the greater memory that this enables, the array in next example extended from 5 to 500.

EXAMPLE 9.2

```
// demo of An array of pointers to objects
#include <iostream.h>
class AIMCA
```

```
{
    public:
        AIMCA() { itsAge = 1; itsWeight=5; }
        ~AIMCA() {} // destructor
        int GetAge() const { return itsAge; }
        int GetWeight() const { return itsWeight; }
        void SetAge(int age) { itsAge = age; }
    private:
        int itsAge;
        int itsWeight;
};

        void main()
    {
    AIMCA * Family[500];
    int i;
    AIMCA * pAimca;
    for (i = 0; i < 500; i++)
    {
        pAimca = new AIMCA;
        pAimca->SetAge(2*i +1);
        Family[i] = pAimca;
    }
    for (i = 0; i < 500; i++)
    {
        cout << "Aimca #" << i+1 << ": ";
        cout << Family[i]->GetAge() << endl;
    }
}
```

9.2.1 A Pointer to an Array Vs an Array of Pointers

Read these three declarations:

1: Child One[500]

2: Child * Two[500];

3: Child * Three = new Child[500];

One is an array of 500 Childs. Two is an array of 500 pointers to Childs. Three is a pointer to an array of 500 Childs.The differences among these three code lines dramatically affect how these arrays operate. What is perhaps even more surprising is that Three is a variant of One, but is very different from Two. This raises the thorny issue of how pointers relate to arrays. In the third case, Three is a pointer to an array. That is, the address in Three is the address of the first item in that array. This is exactly the case for One.

EXAMPLE 9.3

```
#include <iostream.h>
class AITS
{
    public:
       AITS() { itsAge = 1; itsWeight=5; }
       ~AITS();
       int GetAge() const { return itsAge; }
       int GetWeight() const { return itsWeight; }
       void SetAge(int age) { itsAge = age; }
    private:
       int itsAge;
       int itsWeight;
};
    AITS:: ~AITS()
    {
    // cout << "Destructor called!\n";
    }
    void main()
    {
       AITS * Family = new AITS[500];
       int i;
       AIMCA * pAimca;
       for (i = 0; i < 500; i++)
    {
       pAimca = new AITS; // use of new to create a new array member
       pAimca->SetAge(2*i +1);
       Family[i] = *pAimca;
       delete pAimca; //use of delete to release
    }
       for (i = 0; i < 500; i++)
    {
       cout << "Aimca #" << i+1 << ": ";
       cout << Family[i].GetAge() << endl;
    }
       delete [] Family;
}
```

9.2.2 Why Pointers?

To declare a pointer in a program, write the type of the variable or object whose address will be stored in the pointer, followed by the pointer operator (*) and the name of the pointer. For example,

```
int * point = 0;
```

To assign or initialize a pointer, prepend the name of the variable whose address is being assigned with the address of operator (&). For example,

```
int theVar = 5;

int * point = & theVar;
```

To dereference a pointer, prepend the pointer name with the dereference operator (*). For example,

```
int theValue = *point
```

you've seen step-by-step details of assigning a variable's address to a pointer. In practice, though, you would never do this. After all, why bother with a pointer when you already have a variable with access to that value? The only reason for this kind of pointer manipulation of an automatic variable is to demonstrate how pointers work. Pointers are used, most often, for following tasks:

- Managing data on the free store.
- Accessing class member data and functions.
- Passing variables by reference to functions.

9.3 REFERENCE VARIABLE

A reference is work as an alias for an object, when you create a reference, you initialize it with the name of another object. From that moment on, the reference acts as an alternative name for the target object, and anything you do to the reference is really done to the target object.

You can create a reference by writing the type of the target object, followed by the reference operator (&), followed by the name of the reference. References can use any legal variable name. If you have an integer variable named myint, you can make a reference to that variable by writing the following:

```
int &myref = myint;
```

now myref will act as a reference variable for myint in the whole program.

EXAMPLE 9.4

```
// show the use of reference variables

// Demo of References

#include <iostream.h>

void main()

{

    int aone;

    int &ref = aone;
```

```
    aone = 15;
    cout << "AOne: " << aone << endl;
    cout << "ref: " << ref << endl;
    ref = 74;
    cout << "AOne: " << aone << endl;
    cout << "ref: " << ref << endl;
}
```

EXAMPLE 9.5

```
//Use of Address of Operator - & - on References.
#include <iostream.h>
void main()
{
    int intOne;
    int &SomeRef = intOne;
    intOne = 5;
    cout << "intOne: " << intOne << endl;
    cout << "SomeRef: " << SomeRef << endl;
    cout << "&intOne: " << &intOne << endl;
    cout << "&SomeRef: " << &SomeRef << endl;
}
```

9.3.1 References to Objects

You can create a reference to an object, but not to a class. You can not write this:

```
int & intref = int; // wrong
```

You must initialize intref to a particular integer value, such as this:

```
int bignumber = 1200;
int & intref = bignumber;
```

In the same way, you don't initialize a reference to a class like:

```
student & rstu = student; // wrong
```

You must initialize rstu to a particular student object first to set reference like:

```
student nitinpadlia;
student & rstu = nitinpadlia;
```

EXAMPLE 9.6

```
#include <iostream.h>
class SCat
```

```
{
    public:
        SCat (int age, int weight);
        ~SCat() {}
        int GetAge() { return itsAge; }
        int GetWeight() { return itsWeight; }
    private:
        int itsAge;
        int itsWeight;
};
    SCat::SCat(int age, int weight)
{
    itsAge = age;
    itsWeight = weight;
}
    void main()
{
    SCat juli (15,3);
    SCat & rCat = juli;
    cout << "juli is: ";
    cout << juli.GetAge() << " years old. \n";
    cout << "And juli's weight is: ";
    cout << rCat.GetWeight() << " Kg. \n";
}
```

REVIEW QUESTIONS

1. What are the first and last elements in SomeArray[25]?
2. How do you declare a multidimensional array?
3. Initialize the members of the array in Question 2.
4. How many elements are in the array SomeArray[10][5][20]?
5. What is the maximum number of elements that you can add to a linked list?
6. Can you use subscript notation on a linked list?
7. What is the last character in the string "Brad is a nice guy"?
8. What operator is used to determine the address of a variable?
9. What operator is used to find the value stored at an address held in a pointer?
10. What is a pointer?
11. What is the difference between the address stored in a pointer and the value at that address?

12. What is the difference between the indirection operator and the address of operator?
13. What is the difference between const int * ptrOne and int * const ptrTwo?

LAB EXERCISES

1. Declare a two-dimensional array that represents a tic-tac-toe game board.
2. Write the code that initializes all the elements in the array you created in Exercise 1 to the value 0.
3. Write the declaration for a Node class that holds unsigned short integers.
4. What is wrong with this code fragment?

```
unsigned short SomeArray[5][4];
for (int i = 0; i<4; i++)
for (int j = 0; j<5; j++)
SomeArray[i][j] = i+j;
```

5. What is wrong with this code fragment?

```
unsigned short SomeArray[5][4];
for (int i = 0; i<=5; i++)
for (int j = 0; j<=4; j++)
SomeArray[i][j] = 0;
```

6. What do these declarations do?
   (*a*) int * pOne;
   (*b*) int vTwo;
   (c) int * pThree = &vTwo;
7. If you have an unsigned short variable named yourAge, how would you declare a pointer to manipulate yourAge?
8. Assign the value 50 to the variable yourAge by using the pointer that you declared in Exercise 2.
9. Write a small program that declares an integer and a pointer to integer. Assign the address of the integer to the pointer. Use the pointer to set a value in the integer variable.

Chapter 10 INHERITANCE

10.1 INHERITANCE

When you create a class and uses objects to work with class, with a set of attributes and functions, you have created something that is ready to pass these qualities on to it's children or subclass for reuse the main class to save your time and efforts on coding. This is called inheritance, every super class (parent) gives its qualities to its subclass (child).Inheritance in programs made possible to reuse the attributes and functions of a parent class into a child class.

10.1.1 The Family Inheritance

With all family trees we inherit the characteristics of our parents, grand parents and great grand parents. We can inherit that beautiful nose from our mothers side of the family, the buck teeth from our father, the long black hair from our great grandfather etc.

10.1.2 Inheriting Functions and Attributes

The functions and attributes of a class are the combination of two things, its own functions and attributes and the functions r and attributes of all its super classes.A class which adds new functionality to an existing class is said to derive or inherited from that original class. The original class is said to be the new class's base class.

10.1.3 Benefits of Inheritance

- You can reuse your base class functions and attributes in child class, without redifne or retype.
- You can merge functions of multiple classes in a single class, and you will get a new mixed class.

- Your new mobil handset carry many functions of your old one, thus we have to add just few new functions in old handset class.
- In case of windows operating system, all OS uses base classes as inherit class.

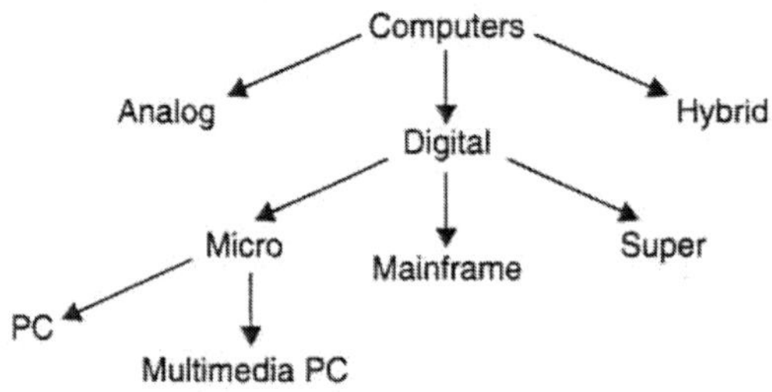

FIGURE 10.1 **Example of Inheritance**

Now From figure you can say a PC inherit the features of MICRO computer, while a MICRO computer inherits the features of a DIGITAL computer and the parent class for all is COMPUTERS.

10.2 TYPES OF INHERITANCE

You can design four type of Inheritance in C++

1. Single level (Parent - Child)
2. Multilevel (Grandparent - Parent - Child)
3. Multiple (Many parents - one child)
4. Hybrid (Mixture of multiple and multilevel)

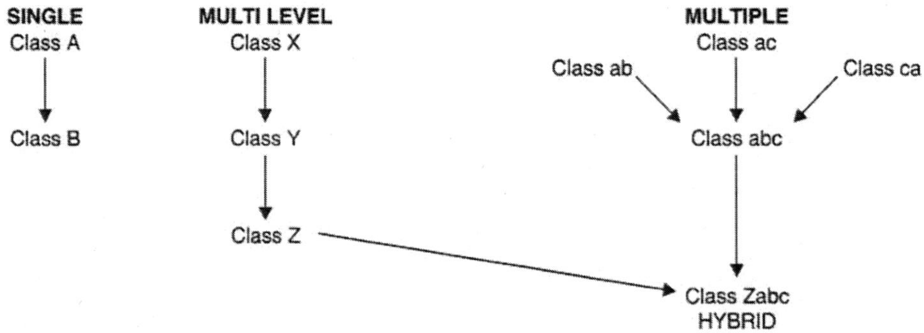

FIGURE 10.2 **Types of inheritance**

10.3 SINGLE LEVEL INHERITANCE

To use single level inheritance in a program you should design a base class or parent class and then child class will inherit it. When you declare a class, you can indicate what class it derives from by writing a colon after the class name, the type of derivation (public or other), and the class from which it derives like:

```
Class child:public parent   // syntax
Class MCA:public amrapali   //example
```

The class from which you derive must have been declared earlier, or you will get a compiler error.

EXAMPLE 10.1

```
//Creation of parent class
class institute
{
char name[25];
int telno;
public:
void getdata()
void showdata();
};
//Creation of child class
class student: public institute
{
int rollno;
char sname[25];
public:
void readdata();
void displaydata();
};
void institute::getdata() //member function of parent class
{
cin>>name;
cin>>telno;
}
void student::readdata() //member function of child class
{
cin>>sname;
cin>>rollno;
}
void institute::showdata() //member function of parent class
{
cout<<name;
cout<<telno;
}
```

```
void student::displaydata() //member function of child class
{
cout<<sname;
cout<<rollno;
}
 // Creation of class objects and function calling
void main
{
student s;
s.getdata() //function of parent class used by child class object
s.readdata();
s.showdata(); //function of parent class used by child class object
s.displaydata();
}
```

10.4 ACCESS SPECIFIERS

There are, in total, three access specifiers:

- public
- protected
- private

all three can be used by a derived class. If a function has an object of your class, it can access all the public member data and functions. The member functions, in turn, can access all private data members and functions of their own class, and all protected data members and functions of any class from which they derive. However, private members are not available to derived classes. Protected data members and functions are fully visible to derived classes, but are otherwise private.

VISIBILITY MODES

Accessible from → ↓ Access mode	Base Class	Derived Class	Outside the class
Public	Y	Y	Y
Private	Y	Y	N
Protected	Y	N	N

FIGURE 10.3 **Table for visibility modes**

10.5 MULTILEVEL INHERITANCE

In some situations classes can be derived more than one level, and we can form of a chain of classes derived by each others.

```
Class win3.11
{

}

class win95:public win3.11
{

}

class win98:public win95
{

}

class win2000:public win98
{

}
```

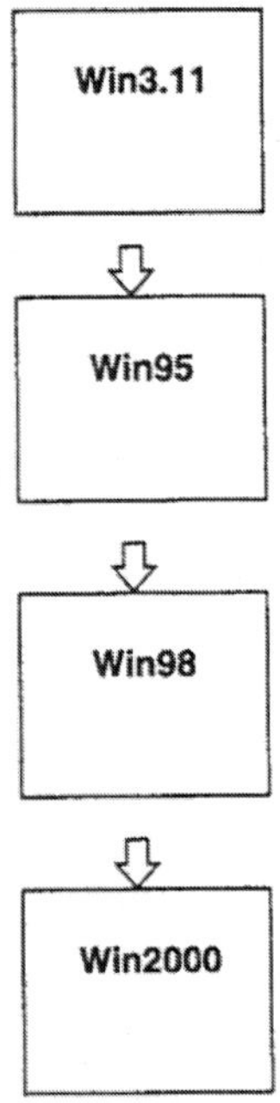

FIGURE 10.4 **Multilevel inheritance in Windows OS**

example and figure shows multilevel inheritance, in that win2000 derived from win98, and win98 is derived from win95 and the parent for all is win3.11 class. That shows win2000 will get the features of earlier parent classes.

10.6 MULTIPLE INHERITANCE

The most common inheritance consists of an object deriving its foundation from another object. This is referred to as single inheritance. C++ allows an object to be based on more than one object. This is called refered to as multiple inheritance. When a class inherits properties or features of more than one base classes, it is known as multiple inheritance. Like:

```
Class a
{
int x,y;
public:
start();
```

```
sum()
getdata()
}
class b
{
int r,l;
public:
move();
setdata();
}
class c
{
float area;
public;
show();
stop();
}
class d:public a, public b, private c //multiple inheritance
{
start();
move();
stop();
final();
}
```

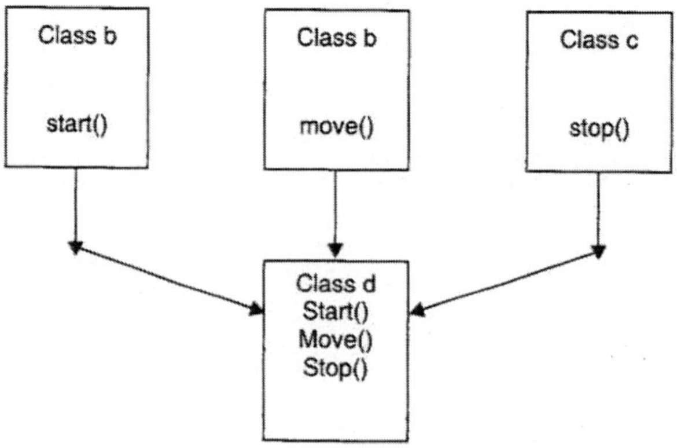

FIGURE 10.5 **Multiple inheritance**

10.7 INHERITANCE OF CONSTRUCTORS AND DESTRUCTORS

When a derived class object is created, his base constructor is called first, creating a parent. Then the derived class constructor is called, completing the construction of the derived class object. When derived class object is destroyed, first the derived class destructor will be called and then the destructor for the parent class will be called. Each destructor is given an opportunity to clean up after its own part of derived class object.

```
 Constructor of Base/parent class
Constructor of Derived /child class
              ...
              .....
              ..
Destructor of Derived /child class
 Destructor of Base /parent class
```

REVIEW QUESTIONS

1. What is inheritance?
2. What are different types of inheritance, describe with examples.
3. How do you show the declaration of a multiple class inheritance?
4. How can you create a virtual copy constructor?
5. How do you invoke a base member function from a derived class in which you've overridden that function?
6. How do you invoke a base member function from a derived class in which you have not overridden that function?
7. If a base class declares a function to be virtual, and a derived class does not use the term virtual when overriding that class, is it still virtual when inherited by a third-generation class?

LAB EXERCISES

1. Show the declaration of class having three float and two integer values with a function that takes an integer parameter and returns void.
2. Show the declaration of a class Square, which derives from Rectangle, which in turn derives from Shape.
3. If, in Exercise 2, Shape takes no parameters, Rectangle takes two (length and width), but Square takes only one (length), show the constructor initialization for Square.
4. Write a constructor for the class Square.
5. What is wrong with this code?

   void SomeFunction (Shape);

   Shape * pRect = new Rectangle;

   SomeFunction(*pRect);

Chapter 11 POLYMORPHISM

11.1 POLYMORPHISM

The word polymorphism has been derived from the greek word Polymorphous. Polus means (Many) and Morphous means (forms), so the meaning of polymorphism is many forms. You can relate polymorphism with synonyms of enlgils language a sinlge word can have multiple meanings. In C language you have already used function, but if you have multiple functions in a C program to perform same type of task you should think individual name for each functions. Using polymorphism C++ solved this problem, now a programmer can define same name functions in a program. Like you want to compute area of a rectangle, circle, triangle you can use area() name for each function. like:

- area(int length, int width) //function for rectangle
- area(int radius) //function for circle
- area(int base, int height) //function for triangle

now you can see that in C++ same name functions can be used to perform different tasks.

11.2 FUNCTION OVERLOADING AND OPERATOR OVERLOADING

In C++ two most popular forms of polymorphism are:

(*a*) Function Overloading

(*b*) Operator Overloading.

11.2.1 Function Overloading

In function overloading a same name functions can be used in a program to perform various tasks like:

- Print(int x)
- Print(char s)
- Print(float y)
- Print (emp e)

The Print() function is overloaded here.

- area(int length, int width) //function for rectangle
- area(int radius) //function for circle
- area(int base, int height) //function for triangle

The area function is overloaded here. You can use area() function to compute area of different shapes like circle or triangle.

On the other hand the meaning of operator overloading is use of single operator like (+ or >>) for different operations. Like:

```
X=a+b; //add two integer values
Name3=sname+fname; // concat two strings
2.35 //use of . operator for decimal place
3.67
emp.name= "mksharma" //use of . operator for object.
```

EXAMPLE 11.1

```
// function overloading example
#include <iostream>
// Rectangle
double MomentOfInertia(double b, double h)
{
    return b * h * h * h / 3;
}
// Semi-Circle
double MomentOfInertia(double R)
{
    const double PI = 3.14159;
    return R * R * R * R * PI/ 8;
}
// Triangle
double MomentOfInertia(double b, double h, int)
```

```
{
    return b * h * h * h / 12;
}
void main()
{
    double base = 7.74, height = 14.38, radius = 12.42;
    cout << "Rectangle\n"<< "Moment of inertia with regard to the
                                X axis: ";
    cout << "I = " << MomentOfInertia(base, height) << "mm\n\n";
    cout << "Semi-Circle\n" << "Moment of inertia with regard to the
                                X axis: ";
    cout << "I = " << MomentOfInertia(radius) << "mm\n\n";
    cout << "Enter the dimensions of the triangle\n";
    cout << "Base: "; cin >> base;
    cout << "Height: "; cin >> height;
    cout << "\nTriangle\n" << "Moment of inertia with regard to the
                                X axis: ";
    cout << "I = " << MomentOfInertia(base, height, 1) << "mm\n\n";
}
```

EXAMPLE 11.2

```
//C++ program to overload function show(), to show different values
using the show() function
#include <iostraem.h>
void show(int val)
{
    cout<<val;
}
void show(double val)
{
    cout<<val;
}
void show(char *val)
{
    cout<< val;
}
void main()
    {
    show(12);
    show(3.1415);
    show("Hello World\n!");
    }
```

11.2.2 Operator Overloading

Operator overloading allows C/C++ operators to have user-defined meaning in user defined class. Overloaded operators are part of C++ polymorphism. If you want to overload a defined operator like + or * to perform some user defined action then, the syntax is:

```
return type operator + (value, values );
return type operator * (value, value);
```

Example:

```
oload operator + (oload, oload); // overloading + operator
oload operator * (oload, oload); // overloading * operator
```

EXAMPLE 11.3

```
class oload {
public:
// Without operator overloading:
oload add(oload, oload);
oload mul(oload, oload);
oload f(oload a, oload b, oload c)
{
return add(add(mul(a,b), mul(b,c)), mul(c,a));
}
// With operator overloading:
oload operator + (oload, oload);
oload operator * (oload, oload);
oload f(oload a, oload b, oload c)
{
return a*b + b*c + c*a;
}
```

11.2.3 Benefits of Operators Overloading

By overloading standard operators on a class, you can exploit the intuition of the users of that class. This lets users program in the language of the problem domain rather than in the language of the machine.

11.2.4 Examples of Operator Overloading

Few of examples of operator overloading:

- myString + yourString might concatenate two string objects
- myDate++ might increment a Date object
- a * b might multiply two Number objects

- a[i] might access an element of an Array object
- x = *p might dereference a "smart pointer" that actually "points" to a disk record

11.2.5 Overloaded Operators

The following operators can be overloaded:

```
+     -     *     /     %     ^     &     |
~     !     ,     =     <     >     <=    >=
++    --    <<    >>    ==    !=    &&    ||
+=    -=    *=    /=    %=    ^=    &=    |=
<<=   >>=   []    ()    ->    ->*   new   delete
```

However, some of these operators may only be overloaded as member functions within a class. This holds true for the '=', the '[]', the '()' and the '->' operators.

11.3 VIRTUAL FUNCTION

A virtual function is a function that makes sure that, in an inheritance scenario, the right function is called regardless of the expression that calls the function. The late or dynamic binding is achieved in C++ with virtual functions. A function becomes virtual when its declaration starts with the keyword virtual. Once a function is declared virtual in a base class, its definition remains virtual in all derived classes; even when the keyword virtual is not repeated in the definition of the derived classes. Like:

```
virtual double Area() const;
virtual void show() const;
virtual void setweight(int wt);
```

EXAMPLE 11.4

```
// C++ program to show the use of virtual function.
class Vehicle
{
    public:
       Vehicle();          // constructors
       Vehicle(int wt);  // interface.. now virtuals!
       virtual int getweight() const;
       virtual void setweight(int wt);
    private:
       int weight;
}
// Vehicle's own getweight() function:
    int Vehicle::getweight() const
```

```
{
    return (weight);
}
class Land: public Vehicle
{
    ...
}
class Auto: public Land
{
...
}
class Truck: public Auto
{
    public:
       Truck(); // constructors
       Truck(int engine_wt, int sp, char const *nm, int trailer_wt);
          // interface: to set two weight fields
       void setweight(int engine_wt, int trailer_wt);
          // and to return combined weight
       int getweight() const;
    private:
       int trailer_weight;
};

// Truck's own getweight() function
int Truck::getweight() const
{
    return (Auto::getweight() + trailer_wt);
}
```

Note that the keyword virtual appears only in the definition of the base class Vehicle; it need not be repeated in the derived classes. The effect of the late binding is:

```
Vehicle
    v(1200); // vehicle with weight 1200
Truck t(6000, 115,"Sawrajmazda", 25000);
Vehicle *vp;
int main()
    { //one
       vp = &v;
       cout<<vp->getweight());
```

```
        //two
        vp = &t;
        cout<<vp->getweight());
        cout<<vp->getspeed());
    }
```

Since the function getweight() is defined as virtual, late binding is used here: in the statements above, just below the one tag, Vehicle's function getweight() is called. In contrast, the statements below tag two use Truck's function getweight().

11.4 VIRTUAL DESTRUCTOR

If you have created a class that is derived from another class. When you dynamically call the inherited class using an instance of the base class, during the closing of the program, the destructor of the child class is called first, followed by the destructor of the base class. If you dynamically declare an instance of the base class and then invoke the children of the class, you need to make sure that each destructor and the right destructor of the classes that was used is called to destroy the class; this is safe measure to avoid memory leak. This aspect of C++ programming is taken care of by declaring the destructor of the base class as virtual. Whenever the destructor of the parent class is declared virtual, the destructor of an inherited class is also virtual. This ensures that, the program closes, all of the destructors of the base class and its children that were used are called, providing a safe claim of the memory that was used. To declare a destructor as virtual, type the virtual keyword on its left, in the body of the class.

EXAMPLE 11.5

```
class Circle
{
public:
    Circle(double r = 0.00);
    virtual ~Circle(); //virtual destructor
    void setradius(const double r) { Radius = r; }
    double getradius() const { return Radius; }
    double Area() const;
    virtual void show() const;
protected:
    double Radius;
};
```

REVIEW QUESTIONS

1. When you overload member functions, in what ways must they differ?
2. What is the difference between function and operator overloading, describe with the help of example?

3. What are the common operators for overload?
4. When is the destructor called?
5. How does the copy constructor differ from the assignment operator (=)?
6. What is the this pointer?
7. How do you differentiate between overloading the prefix and postfix increment operators?
8. Can you overload the operator+ for short integers?
9. Is it legal in C++ to overload the operator++ so that it decrements a value in your class?
10. What return value must conversion operators have in their declarations?

LAB EXERCISES

1. Write a SimpleCircle class declaration (only) with one member variable: itsRadius. Include a default constructor, a destructor, and accessor methods for radius.
2. Using the class you created in Exercise 1, write the implementation of the default constructor, initializing itsRadius with the value 5.
3. Using the same class, add a second constructor that takes a value as its parameter and assigns that value to itsRadius.
4. Create a prefix and postfix increment operator for your SimpleCircle class that increments itsRadius.
5. Change SimpleCircle to store itsRadius on the free store, and fix the existing methods.
6. Provide a copy constructor for SimpleCircle.
7. Provide an assignment operator for SimpleCircle.
8. Write a program that creates two SimpleCircle objects. Use the default constructor on one and instantiate the other with the value.
9. Call the increment operator on each and then print their values. Finally, assign the second to the first and print its values.

Chapter 12

STREAMS AND FILES

12.1 COUT<< REDEFINE

The cout<< function is a part of standard C++ library, is a common way for a program to display data on-screen. You've already seen cout<< used in many of the examples earlier. Now you will to see how cout<< works.Printing a text message on-screen is simple. All the cout<< function, passing the desired message enclosed in double quotation marks. For example, to display Hello World on-screen use:

```
cout<<"Hello World ";
```

In addition to text messages, however, you frequently need to display the value of program variables. This is a little more complichilded than displaying only a message. For example, suppose you want to display the value of the numeric variable a on-screen, along with some identifying text. Furthermore, you want the information to start at the beginning of a new line. You could use the cout<< function as follows:

```
cout<<"\nThe value of a is "<< a;
```

12.2 ESCAPE SEQUENCES

Sequence	Meaning
\a	Bell (alert)
\b	Backspace
\n	Newline
\t	Horizontal tab
\\	Backslash
\?	Question mark
\'	Single quotation

Escape sequences are used to control the lochildion of output by moving the screen cursor. They are also used to print characters that would otherwise have a special meaning to cout<<). For example, to print a single backslash character, include a double backslash (\\) in the format string. The first backslash tells cout<<) that the second backslash is to be interpreted as a literal character, not as the start of an escape sequence. In general, the backslash tells cout<<) to interpret the next character in a special manner. Here are some examples:

EXAMPLE 12.1

```
/* Demo of frequently used escape sequences */
#include <stdio.h>
#define QUIT 3
int get_menu_choice( void );
void print_report( void );
void main()
{
    int choice = 0;
    while (choice != QUIT)
    {
       choice = get_menu_choice();
       if (choice == 1)
          cout<<"\nBeeping the computer\a\a\a" );
       else
    {
       if (choice == 2)
          print_report();
    }
}
cout<<"You chose to quit!\n");
    }
    int get_menu_choice( void )
    {
       int selection = 0;
       do
    {
       cout<< "\n" );
       cout<< "\n1 - Beep Computer" );
       cout<< "\n2 - Display Report");
       cout<< "\n3 - Quit");
       cout<< "\n" );
       cout<< "\nEnter a selection:");
```

```
    cin>>selection;
} while ( selection < 1 || selection > 3 );
return selection;
}
void print_report( void )
{
    cout<< "\nSAMPLE REPORT");
    cout<< "\n\nSequence\tMeaning");
    cout<< "\n=========\t=======");
    cout<< "\n\\a\t\tbell (alert)");
    cout<< "\n\\b\t\tbackspace");
    cout<< "\n...\t\t...");
}
```

12.3 STREAMS IN C++

Using the iostream.h C++ view the flow of data from your program to the screen as being a stream of data that is one byte following another. If the destination of the stream is a file or the screen, the source is usually some part of your program. If the stream is reversed, the data can come from the keyboard or a disk file and be "poured" into your data variables.

Data value ......>input stream ....> variable in memory / file

Data value in memory .....>output stream ....>screen / printer / file

One principal goal of streams is to encapsulate the problems of getting the data to and from the disk or the screen. Once a stream is created, your program works with the stream and the stream control e details.

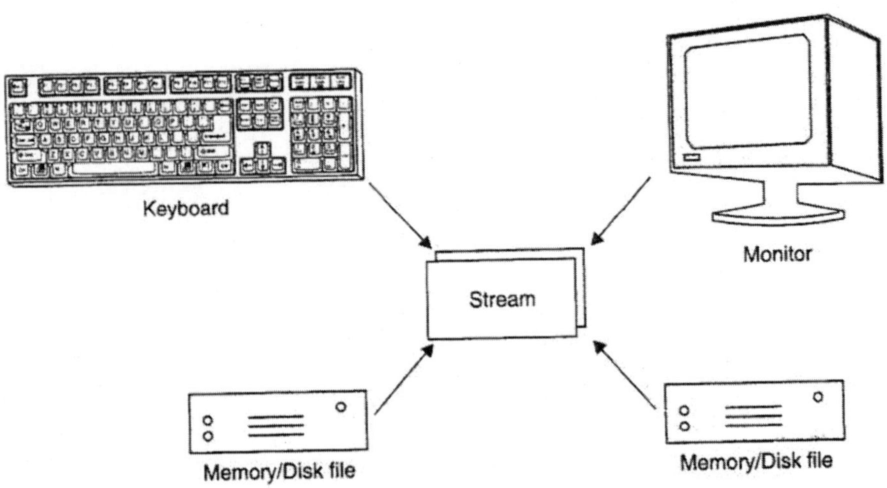

FIGURE 12.1 **Streams in C++**

12.4 BUFFERS IN C++

Writing some data to the disk or to screen is very "expensive." It takes a long time to write data to the disk or to read data from the disk, and execution of the program is generally blocked by disk writes and reads. To solve this problem, streams provide "buffering." Data is written into the stream, but it is not written back out to the disk immediately. Instead, the stream's buffer fills and fills, and when it is full it writes to the disk all at once.C++ takes an object-oriented view toward implementing streams and buffers. The streambuf class manages the buffer, and its member functions provide the capability to fill, empty, flush, and otherwise manipulate the buffer. The ios class is the base class to the input and output stream classes. The ios class has a streambuf object as a member variable. The istream and ostream classes derive from the ios class and specialize input and output stream behavior, respectively. The iostream class is derived from both the istream and the ostream classes and provides input and output methods for writing to the screen. The fstream classes provide input and output from files.

12.5 OBJECTS OF IOSTREAM CLASS

Every C++ program that includes the iostream classes has four objects that are created and initialized. When iostream class library is added to your program you can use all the functions to put the appropriate include statement at the top of your program listing. Like:

cin: handles input from the standard input, the keyboard.

cout: handles output to the standard output, the screen.

cer: handles un buffered output to the standard error device, the screen. Because this is un buffered, everything sent to cerr is written to the standard error device immediately, without waiting for the buffer to fill or for a flush command to be received.

clog: handles buffered error messages that are output to the standard error device, the screen. It is common for this to be "redirected" to a log file, as described in the following section.

12.5.1 Read Data Values

The object cin is responsible for read or input data values and is made available to your program when you include iostream.h. Using the overloaded extraction operator (>>) cin can put data into your program's variables. Like:

```
int someVariable;

cout << "Enter a number: ";

cin >> someVariable;
```

You should learn now that cin can overloaded the extraction operator for a great variety of parameters, among them int&, short&, long&, double&, float&, char&, char*, and so forth. When you write:

cin >> someVariable;

the type of someVariable is assessed. In the example above, someVariable is an integer, so the following function is called:

```
istream & operator>> (int &)
```

Note that because the parameter is passed by reference, the extraction operator is able to act on any type of C++ original variable like:

EXAMPLE 12.2

```
#include <iostream.h>
void main()
{
    int myInt;
    long myLong;
    double myDouble;
    float myFloat;
    unsigned int myUnsigned;
    cout << "int: ";
    cin >> myInt;
    cout << "Long: ";
    cin >> myLong;
    cout << "Double: ";
    cin >> myDouble;
    cout << "Float: ";
    cin >> myFloat;
    cout << "Unsigned: ";
    cin >> myUnsigned;
    cout << "\n\nInt:\t" << myInt << endl;
    cout << "Long:\t" << myLong << endl;
    cout << "Double:\t" << myDouble << endl;
    cout << "Float:\t" << myFloat << endl;
    cout << "Unsigned:\t" << myUnsigned << endl;
}
```

12.5.2 String Handling Problem

Using cin, when you will try to enter a full name into a string. cin believes that white space is a separator. When it sees a space or a new line, it assumes the input for the parameter is complete, and in the case of strings it adds a null character right then and there and you can not input two strings separated using simple cin like "mk sharma". In above example you can check it.

EXAMPLE 12.3

```
// string problem using cin
#include <iostream.h>
void main()
{
    char YourName[50];
    cout << "Your first name: ";
    cin >> YourName;
    cout << "Here it is: " << YourName << endl;
    cout << "Your Full name: ";
    cin >> YourName;
    cout << "Here it is: " << YourName << endl;
}
```

Output: Your first name: Mahesh

Here it is: Mahesh

Your Full name: Mahesh Kumar Sharma

Here it is: Mahesh Kumar Sharma

12.5.3 Get() with cin

The cin Operator >> taking a character reference can be used to get a single character, multiple characters or strings from the standard input. That you will check in given examples:

EXAMPLE 12.4

```
#include <iostream.h>
void main()
{
    char ch;
    while ( (ch = cin.get()) != EOF)
    {
    cout << "ch: " << ch << endl;
    }
    cout << "\nDone!\n";
}
```

to exit this program, you must send end of file from the keyboard. On DOS /windows computers use Ctrl+Z.

World

ch: W

ch: o

ch: r

ch: l

ch: d

ch:

(ctrl-z)

Done!

EXAMPLE 12.5

```
// Read multiple characters with cin
void main()
{
    char a, b, c;
    cout << "Enter three letters: ";
    cin.get(a).get(b).get(c);
    cout << "a: " << a << "\nb: " << b << "\nc: " << c << endl;
}
```

Output: Enter three letters: mks

a: m

b: k

c: s

EXAMPLE 12.6

```
//Read strings with cin
void main()
{
    char stringOne[256];
    char stringTwo[256];
    cout << "Enter string one: ";
    cin.get(stringOne,256);
    cout << "stringOne: " << stringOne << endl;
    cout << "Enter string two: ";
    cin >> stringTwo;
    cout << "StringTwo: " << stringTwo << endl;
}
```

Output: Enter string one: My name is mks

stringOne: My name is mks

Enter string two: What is yours

StringTwo: What

12.5.4 getline(), putline()

When a user want to enter a string, and that string can be read by getline(). Like get(), getline() takes a buffer and a maximum number of characters. Unlike get(), however, the terminating newline is read and thrown away. With get() the terminating newline is not thrown away. It is left in the input buffer. You can use putline() to print the string on screen with spaces.

EXAMPLE 12.7

```
#include <iostream.h>
void main()
{
    char sOne[256];
    char sTwo[256];
    char sThree[256];
    cout << "Enter string one: ";
    cin.getline(sOne,256);
    cout << "stringOne: " << sOne << endl;
    cout << "Enter string two: ";
    cin >> sTwo;
    cout << "stringTwo: " << sTwo << endl;
    cout << "Enter string three: ";
    cin.getline(sThree,256);
    cout << "stringThree: " << sThree << endl;
}
```

Output: Enter string one: one two three

stringOne: one two three

Enter string two: four five six

stringTwo: four

Enter string three: stringThree: five six

12.5.5 ignore(), peek() and putback()

Any times you want to ignore the remaining characters on a line until you hit either end of line (EOL) or end of file (EOF). The member function ignore() serves this purpose. ignore() takes two parameters, the maximum number of characters to ignore and the termination character. If you write ignore(80,'\n'), up to 80 characters will be thrown away until a newline character is found. The input object cin has two additional methods that can be used in some programs peek(), which looks at but does not extract the next character, and putback(), which inserts a character into the input stream.

EXAMPLE 12.8

```
#include <iostream.h>
void main()
{
    char ch;
    cout << "enter a phrase: ";
    while ( cin.get(ch) )
    {
    if (ch == '!')
       cin.putback('$');
    else
       cout << ch;
    while (cin.peek() == '#')
       cin.ignore(1,'#');
    }
}
```

Output: enter a phrase: Now!is#the!time#for!fun#!

Now$isthe$timeforfun

12.5.6 put(), write()

You have used cout along with the overloaded insertion operator (<<) to write strings, integers, and other numeric data to the screen. It is also possible to format the data, aligning columns and writing the numeric data in decimal and hexadecimal. Just as the extraction operator can be supplemented with get() and getline(), the insertion operator can be supplemented with put() and write().The function put() is used to write a single character to the output device. Because put() returns an ostream reference, and because cout is an ostream object, you can concatenate put() just as you do the insertion operator.

EXAMPLE 12.9

```
// use of put with cout
#include <iostream.h>
void main()
{
    cout.put('H').put('e').put('l').put('l').put('o').put('\n');
}
```

Output: Hello

EXAMPLE 12.10

```
// program to show the use of write() function with cout
#include <iostream.h>
#include <string.h>
void main()
{
    char One[] = "India is my land";
    int fullLength = strlen(One);
    int tooShort = fullLength -7;
    int tooLong = fullLength + 5;
    cout.write(One,fullLength) << "\n";
    cout.write(One,tooShort) << "\n";
    cout.write(One,tooLong) << "\n";
}
```

Output: India is my motherland

India is

India is my motherland i?!.!

12.5.7 width(), fill()

The default width of your output will be just enough space to print the number, character, or string in the output buffer. You can change this by using width(). Normally cout fills the empty field created by a call to width() with spaces. At times you may want to fill the area with other characters, such as asterisks or +. To do this, you call fill() and pass in as a parameter the character you want used as a fill character. Like:

EXAMPLE 12.11

```
#include <iostream.h>
void main()
{
    cout << "aimca >";
    cout.width(25);
    cout << courses << "< MCA\n";
    cout << "aimca >";
    cout.width(25);
    cout.fill('*');
    cout << courses << "< MBA\n";
}
```

Output: aimca > courses< MCA

aimca >******************courses< MBA

12.5.8 setf()

The iostream objects keep track of their state by using flags. You can set these flags by calling setf() and passing in one or another of the predefined enumerated constants. For example, you can set whether or not to show trailing zeros (so that 20.00 does not become truncated to 20). To turn trailing zeros on, use setf(ios::showpoint).You can turn on the plus sign (+) before positive numbers by using ios::showpos. You can change the alignment of the output by using ios::left, ios::right, or ios::internal.Finally, you can set the base of the numbers for display by using ios::dec (decimal), ios::oct (octal—base eight), or ios::hex (hexadecimal—base sixteen). Like:

EXAMPLE 12.12

```
#include <iostream.h>
#include <iomanip.h>
void main()
{
    const int number = 185;
    cout << "The number is " << number << endl;
    cout << "The number is " << hex << number << endl;
    cout.setf(ios::showbase);
    cout << "The number is " << hex << number << endl;
    cout << "The number is ";
    cout.width(10);
    cout << hex << number << endl;
    cout << "The number is ";
    cout.width(10);
    cout.setf(ios::left);
    cout << hex << number << endl;
    cout << "The number is ";
    cout.width(10);
    cout.setf(ios::internal);
    cout << hex << number << endl;
    cout << "The number is:" << setw(10) << hex << number << endl;
}
```

12.6 FILE STREAMS

File Stream provide a uniform way of dealing with data coming from the hard disk and going out to the screen or printer or coming from the keyboard and going to hard disk. In either case, you can use the insertion and extraction operators with file stream objects with related functions. To open and close files, you have ofstraem, ifstream and fstream objects.

- Ofstraem : to write into files
- Ifstream : to read from files
- Fstream : both read and write

12.6.1 Ofstream and Ifstream

The ofstream used to read from or write to files are called ofstream objects. These are derived from the iostream objects you've been using so far. To get started with writing to a file, you must first create an ofstream object, and then associate that object with a particular file on your disk. To use ofstream objects, you must be sure to include fstream.h in your program.

While the ifstream is used read data values from a file. To get started to read from a file, you must first create an ifstream object, and then associate that object with a particular file on your disk. To open the file myfile.txt with an ofstream object, declare an instance of an ofstream object and pass in the filename as a parameter:

```
ofstream fout("myfile.txt");
```

Opening this file for input works exactly the same way, except it uses an ifstream object:

```
ifstream fin("myfile.txt");
```

EXAMPLE 12.13

```
#include <fstream.h>
void main()
{
    char fileName[80];
    char buffer[255]; // for user input
    cout << "Enter File name: ";
    cin >> fileName;
    ofstream fout(fileName); // open for writing
    fout << "This line written directly to the file...\n";
    cout << "Enter text for the file: ";
    cin.ignore(1,'\n'); // ignore the newline after the file name
    cin.getline(buffer,255); // get the user's input
    fout << buffer << "\n"; // and write it to the file
    fout.close(); // close the file, ready for reopen
    ifstream fin(fileName); // reopen for reading
    cout << "Here's the contents of the file:\n";
    char ch;
    while (fin.get(ch))
    cout << ch;
    cout << "\n***End of file ***\n";
    fin.close(); // close the file stream
}
```

12.7 FILE OPENING MODES

The default behavior upon opening a file is to create the file if it doesn't yet exist and to truncate the file or delete all its contents if it does exist. If you don't want this default behavior, you can explicitly provide a second argument to the constructor of your ofstream object.Valid arguments include:

- **ios::app** —Appends to the end of existing files rather than truncating them.
- **ios::at** —Places you at the end of the file, but you can write data anywhere in the file.
- **ios::trun** —The default. Causes existing files to be truncated.
- **ios::nocreat** —If the file does not exist, the open fails.
- **ios::noreplac** —If the file does already exist, the open fails.

Note that app is short for append; ate is short for at end, and trunc is short for truncate.

EXAMPLE 12.14

```
// program to show the Appending of data at the end of a file
#include <fstream.h>
void main()
{
    char fileName[80];
    char buffer[255];
    cout << "Please re-enter the file name: ";
    cin >> fileName;
    ifstream fin(fileName);
    if (fin) // already exists?
{
    cout << "Current file contents:\n";
    char ch;
    while (fin.get(ch))
    cout << ch;
    cout << "\n***End of file contents.***\n";
}
fin.close();
cout << "\nOpening " << fileName << " in append mode...\n";
ofstream fout(fileName,ios::app);
if (!fout)
{
    cout << "Unable to open " << fileName << " for appending.\n";
    return(1);
}
```

```
cout << "\nEnter text for the file: ";
cin.ignore(1,'\n');
cin.getline(buffer,255);
fout << buffer << "\n";
fout.close();
fin.open(fileName); // reassign existing fin object!
if (!fin)
{
    cout << "Unable to open " << fileName << " for reading.\n";
    return(1);
}
cout << "\nHere's the contents of the file:\n";
char ch;
while (fin.get(ch))
cout << ch;
cout << "\n***End of file contents.***\n";
fin.close();
}
```

12.8 TEXT VS BINARY FILES

Operating systems, such as DOS or Windows, distinguish between text files and binary files. Text files store everything as text large numbers such as 54,325 are stored as a string of numerals ('5', '4', ',', '3', '2', '5'). This can be inefficient, but has the advantage that the text can be read using simple programs such as the DOS command type or Unix command cat or in Windows using notepad. Today there is a need to store images, sounds, video in a file form. To help this file system distinguish between text and binary files, C++ provides the ios::binary flag to create binary files. On many systems, this flag is ignored because all data is stored in binary format. Binary files can store not only integers and strings, but entire data structures or class can be write or read at once in a binary file using write() and read() methods. Like in a class employee to write or read an object you can use:

```
fout.write(char* &name of object,sizeof (object));
fout.write(char* &emp,sizeof (emp));
fout.read(char* &name of object,sizeof (object));
fout.read(char* &emp,sizeof (emp));
```

Each of these functions expects a pointer to character, however, so you must cast the address of your class to be a pointer to character.The second argument to these functions is the number of characters to write, which you can determine using sizeof() function.

EXAMPLE 12.15

```
// program to write and read data of an employee in text file
#include <fstream.h>
#include <iostream.h>
#include <string.h>
void main()
{
char FileName[20];
char EName[40], Address[50], City[20], State[32], pinCode[10];
    cout << "Enter the Following pieces of information\n";
    cout << "Employee Name: ";
    cin.getline(EName, 40);
    cout << "Address: ";
    cin.getline(Address, 50);
    cout << "City: ";
    cin.getline(City, 20);
    cout << "State: ";
    cin.getline(State, 32);
    cout << "Pin Code: ";
    cin.getline(pinCode, 10);
    cout << "\nEnter the name of the file you want to create: ";
    cin >> FileName;
    ofstream EmplRecords(FileName, ios::out);
    EmplRecords << EName << "\n" << Address << "\n" << City
    << "\n" << State << "\n" << ZIPCode;
    cout << "Enter the name of the file you want to open: ";
    cin >> FileName;
    ifstream EmplRecords(FileName);
    EmplRecords.getline(EName, 40, '\n');
    EmplRecords.getline(Address, 50);
    EmplRecords.getline(City, 20);
    EmplRecords.getline(State, 32);
    EmplRecords.getline(ZIPCode, 10);
    cout << "\n -=- Employee Information -=-";
    cout << "\nEmpl Name: " << EName;
    cout << "\nAddress: " << Address;
    cout << "\nCity: " << City;
    cout << "\nState: " << State;
cout << "\nZIP Code: " << ZIPCode;
cout << "\n\n";
}
```

EXAMPLE 12.16

```
//program to write a block of class object and read with the help of
write() and read function
#include <fstream.h>
class Animal
{
public: //constructor defined
Animal(int weight, long days):itsWeight(weight),itsNumberDays
Alive(days){}
    ~Animal(){} // use of destructor
    int GetWeight()const { return itsWeight; }
    void SetWeight(int weight) { itsWeight = weight; }
    long GetDaysAlive()const { return itsNumberDaysAlive; }
    void SetDaysAlive(long days) { itsNumberDaysAlive = days; }
private:
    int itsWeight;
    long itsNumberDaysAlive;
};
void main()
{
    char fileName[80];
    char buffer[255];
    cout << "Please enter the file name: ";
    cin >> fileName;
    ofstream fout(fileName,ios::binary);
    if (!fout)
    {
    cout << "Unable to open " << fileName << " for writing.\n";
    return(1);
    }
    Animal Dog(50,30);
    fout.write((char*) &Dog,sizeof Dog);
    fout.close();
    ifstream fin(fileName,ios::binary);
    if (!fin)
    {
       cout << "Unable to open " << fileName << " for reading.\n";
       return(1);
    }
```

```
        Animal DogTwo(1,1);
        cout << "DogTwo weight: " << DogTwo.GetWeight() << endl;
        cout << "DogTwo days: " << DogTwo.GetDaysAlive() << endl;
        fin.read((char*) &DogTwo, sizeof DogTwo);
        cout << "DogTwo weight: " << DogTwo.GetWeight() << endl;
        cout << "DogTwo days: " << DogTwo.GetDaysAlive() << endl;
        fin.close();
    }
```

12.9 COMMAND LINE PROCESSING

Many operating systems, like DOS and UNIX, enable the user to pass parameters to your program when the program starts. These are called command-line options, and are typically separated by spaces on the command line. For example:

```
C:\>Copy file1 file2 //DOS copy command
$cp file1 file2 //Unix copy command
```

These parameters are not passed to main() directly. Instead, every program's main() function is passed two parameters. The first is an integer count of the number of arguments on the command line. The program name itself is counted, so every program has at least one parameter. The example command line shown previously has 3. The second parameter passed to main() is an array of pointers to character strings. Because an array name is a constant pointer to the first element of the array, you can declare this argument to be a pointer to a pointer to char, a pointer to an array of char, or an array of arrays of char.

```
void main(int argc, char *argv[])
```

Typically, the first argument is called argc (argument count), but you may call it anything you like. The second argument is often called argv (argument vector), but again this is just a convention.It is common to test argc to ensure you've received the expected number of arguments, and to use argv to access the strings themselves. Note that argv[0] is the name of the program, and argv[1] is the first parameter to the program, represented as a string. If your program takes two numbers as arguments, you will need to translate these numbers to strings.

EXAMPLE 12.17

```
// Write a simple C++ program to show the use of command line
parameters
#include <iostream.h>
void main(int argc, char *argv[])
{
    cout << "Received " << argc << " arguments...\n";
    for (int i=0; i<argc; i++)
       cout << "argument " << i << ": " << argv[i] << endl;
}
```

Output: Object oriented programming in C++
Received 5 arguments...
argument 0: Object
argument 1: oriented
argument 2: programming
argument 3: in
argument 4: C++

REVIEW QUESTIONS

1. What is a stream, how can you differ input stream and output stream?
2. What is fstream, and what does it do?
3. What are the three forms of cin.get(), and what are their differences?
4. What is the difference between cin.read() and cin.getline()?
5. What are the different file opening modes?
6. Write about command line parameters.
7. What is a ofstream object?
8. What does the ios::app argument do?

LAB EXERCISES

1. Write a program that writes to the four standard iostream objects: cin, cout, cerr, and clog.
2. Write a program that prompts the user to enter her full name and then displays it on the screen.
3. Write program to write data of 10 books in a binary file and then read all.
4. Write a program that takes a filename as a parameter and opens the file for reading. Read every character of the file and display only the letters and punctuation to the screen. (Ignore all nonprinting characters.) Then close the file and exit.
5. Write a program that displays its command-line arguments in reverse order and does not display the program name.
6. Write program to count total characters in a text file.
7. Make a small project use binary file to perform following operations:
   Add records
   Display all records
   Search a record
   Delete a record
   Update a record
8. Write a program to copy a text file into new text file.

Chapter 13

FRIEND CLASSES, FRIEND FUNCTIONS AND INLINE FUNCTIONS

13.1 FRIEND CLASS

A class can be made a friend of another class. When class A is made a friend of class B, all members of class B are directly accessible to the members of class A; this includes private (and protected) members. Friendship is not mutual: the fact that class A is made a friend of class B does not imply that class B is made a friend of class A. In other words, the fact that the (private and protected) members of class B are accessible to the members of class A does not mean that the members of class A area accessible to the members of class B. If you want to expose your private member data or functions to another class, you must declare that class to be a friend. This extends the interface of your class to include the friend class.To make one class a friend of another, in the body of the class that is granting the friendship, type:-

```
friend class ClassName;
```

The keywords friend and class are required. The ClassName is the name of the class that needs friendship. Here is an example: -

EXAMPLE 13.1

```
class Dimensions
{
    friend class Labels;
    public:
       Dimensions(Double L = 0.00, Double W = 0.00);
       ~Dimensions();
       void setDimensions(const Double L, const Double H);
       Double getLength() const { return Length; }
```

```
        Double getHeight() const { return Height; }
        Double Area() const;
    private:
        Double Length;
        Double Height;
};
```

13.2 FRIEND FUNCTION

Good programming techniques are that in which you should hide the variables used to store data of a class. This is done by declaring the member variables in the private section. Once a variable is hidden like that, only the members of the same class have access to it. The C++ language provides an alternative to this problem. Although you can still hide your variables, you can create special functions that have a "priviledged" access to the members of the private section of a class. These functions are not members of the class, they are just granted special access to the hidden member variables. Such functions are qualified as friend functions.

```
friend double TotalPrice(objectname i);
```

To declare a friend function, start with the friend keyword, followed by the return value, followed by the name of the function, its parentheses, and possibly the necessary arguments. Since a friend is not a function member of the object, you should provide access to the object, one way or another. When a function has been declared as a friend of a class, the class grants and controls the friendship.

The friend keyword is used only when declaring the friendly function. When defining the function, proceed as if it were a regularly declared function, omitting the friend keyword. Because friend functions are given special access, they can be declared anywhere in the class; but a good habit is to postion them on top of the object just under the opening curly bracket. This allow the compiler, yo, and anybody who reads your code to have the list of friends of the class.

EXAMPLE 13.2

```
#include <iostream.h>
class Student
{
    friend Student Registration();
    public:
    Student();
    Student(string FN, string LN);
    Student(string fn, string ln, int d, int m, int y);
    Student(const Student& S);
    ~Student();
    void setFirstName(string f) { FirstName = f; }
    string getFirstName() { return FirstName; }
```

```
    void setLastName(string l) { LastName = l; }
    string getLastName() { return LastName; }
    void setDayOfBirth(int d) { DayOfBirth = d; }
    int getDayOfBirth() { return DayOfBirth; }
    void setMonthOfBirth(int m) { MonthOfBirth = m; }
    int getMonthOfBirth() { return MonthOfBirth; }
    void setYearOfBirth(int y) { YearOfBirth = y; }
    int getYearOfBirth() { return YearOfBirth; }
    private:
    string FirstName;
    string LastName;
    int DayOfBirth;
    int MonthOfBirth;
    int YearOfBirth;
};
    Student Registration()
{
    Student S;
    // Notice that the function has access to the
    // private members of the class
    cout << "Enter the student's information\n";
    cout << "First Name: "; cin >> S.FirstName;
    cout << "Last Name: "; cin >> S.LastName;
    cout << "Day of Birth: "; cin >> S.DayOfBirth;
    cout << "Month of Birth: "; cin >> S.MonthOfBirth;
    cout << "Year of Birth: "; cin >> S.YearOfBirth;
    return S;
}
Student::Student()
{
    FirstName = "Jyoti";
    LastName = "Pandey";
    DayOfBirth = 21;
    MonthOfBirth = 4;
    YearOfBirth = 1983;
}
    Student::Student(string FN, string LN)
    : FirstName(FN), LastName(LN),
```

```
    DayOfBirth(1), MonthOfBirth(1), YearOfBirth(1990)
{

}
Student::Student(string fn, string ln, int d, int m, int y)
    : FirstName(fn), LastName(ln),
    DayOfBirth(d), MonthOfBirth(m), YearOfBirth(y)
{
}
Student::Student(const Student& Stud)
    : FirstName(Stud.FirstName),
    LastName(Stud.LastName),
    DayOfBirth(Stud.DayOfBirth),
    MonthOfBirth(Stud.MonthOfBirth),
    YearOfBirth(Stud.YearOfBirth)
{
}
Student::~Student()
{
cout<< "End of objects";
}
#include <iostream.h>
void main(int argc, char* argv[])
{
    TStudent Stud;
    void StudentInfo(TStudent Grade1);
    Stud = Registration();
    StudentInfo(Stud);
}
void StudentInfo(TStudent s)
{
    cout << "\nStudent Registration";
    cout << "\nFull Name: "
    << s.getFirstName() << " " << s.getLastName();
    cout << "\nDate of Birth: " << s.getDayOfBirth() << "/"
    << s.getMonthOfBirth() << "/" << s.getYearOfBirth();
}
```

13.3 INLINE FUNCTION

When you define a function, normally the compiler creates just one set of instructions in memory. When you call the function, execution of the program jumps to those instructions, and when the function returns, execution jumps back to the next line in the calling function. If you call the function 5 times, your program jumps to the same set of instructions each time. This means there is only one copy of the function, not 5.There is some performance overhead in jumping in and out of functions. It turns out that some functions are very small, just a line or two of code, and some efficiency can be gained if the program can avoid making these jumps just to execute one or two instructions. The program runs faster if the function call can be avoided. If a function is declared with the keyword inline, the compiler does not create a real function: it copies the code from the inline function directly into the calling function. No jump is made; it is just as if you had written the statements of the function right into the calling function. To declare a function inline use the keyword inline before the type of function. **Inline returntype functionname(passing parameter)**

```
inline int double(int);
```

An inline function is a function whose code gets inserted into the caller's code stream. Like a #define macro, inline functions improve performance by avoiding the overhead of the call itself and (especially!) by the compiler being able to optimize through the call.

EXAMPLE 13.3

```
// inline function two compute squre aad cube of integer numbers
#include <iostream.h>
inline double squre(int);
inline double cube(int)
void main()
{
    int num;
    double sq,cub;
    cout << "Enter a number ";
    cin >> num;
    cout << "\n";
    sq = squre(num);
    cout << "Squre is:" <<sq << endl;
    cub = cube(num);
    cout << "Cube is: " << cub << endl;
}
    double squre(int num)
{
    return num*num;
}
    double cube(int num)
{
    return num*num*num;
}
```

REVIEW QUESTIONS

1. How do you define a friend class, give suitable example?
2. How do you define a friend function, explain with the help of a example?
3. What is the difference between friend function and friend class?
4. What is the difference between inline function and friend function?
5. What is a virtual friend function?
6. What is a virtual friend class?

LAB EXERCISES

1. Show the declaration of a class, Aimca, that contains a data member that is a string object.
2. Show the declaration of a class, with two inline function to add and multiply four numbers.
3. Show the declaration of a friend function which will use marks from 5 classes and then it will add all.

Chapter 14

EXCEPTIONS AND ERROR HANDLING

14.1 AN EXCEPTION

In C++, an exception is an object that is passed from the area of code where a logical problem occurs to the part of the code that is going to handle the problem like divide by zero or squre root of a negative number. The type of the exception determines which area of code will handle the problem, and the contents of the object thrown, if any, may be used to provide warning to the user and terminate the program instead to work in an infinite loop that cause crash of system. Exceptions are an integral and unavoidable part of the operating system and programming. In good software design it is must to provide exception handling functions. C++ exception handling provides a type-safe, integrated method for coping with the predictable but unusual conditions that arise while running a program. Like out of memory or divide by zero or reading a string in place of integer value.

14.2 BASICS OF EXCEPTIONS HANDLING

The basic idea behind exceptions handling in a computer program that is integral part of a software is:

The actual allocation of resources like memory or the locking of a file is usually done at a very low level in the program. The logic of what to do when an operation fails, memory cannot be allocated, or a file cannot be open is usually high in a large program with the code for interacting with the user. Exceptions provide an express path from the code that allocates resources to the code that can handle the error condition. If there are intervening layers of functions, they are given an opportunity to clean up memory allocations, but are not required to include code whose only purpose is to pass along the error condition.

The basic steps in using exceptions are:

- Identify those areas of the program in which you begin an operation that might raise an exception, and put them in try blocks like long divisions.
- Create catch blocks to catch the exceptions if they are thrown, to clean up allocated memory, and to warn the user as appropriate. A common try.. catch block syntax is:

```
try
{
function();
throw integer;
}
catch(OutOfMemory)
{
// take some actions
}

catch(FileNotFound)
{
// take other action
}
```

To catch exceptions you must place a portion of code under exception inspection. This is done by enclosing that portion of code in a *try block*. When an exceptional circumstance arises within that block, an exception is thrown that transfers the control to the exception handler. If no exception is thrown, the code continues normally and all handlers are ignored.

A exception is thrown by using the throw keyword from inside the try block. Exception handlers are declared with the keyword catch, which must be placed immediately after the try block like:

```
#include <iostream.h>
void main ()
{
try
    {
    throw 20;
    }
    catch (int e)
    {
       cout << "An exception occurred. Exception Nr. " << e << endl;
    }
}
```

A throw expression accepts one parameter (in this case the integer value 20), which is passed as an argument to the exception handler. The exception handler is declared with the catch keyword. As you can see, it follows immediately the closing brace of the try block. The catch format is similar to a regular function that always has at least one parameter. The type of this parameter is very important, since the type of the argument passed by the throw expression is checked against it, and only in the case they match, the exception is catch.

14.3 MULTIPLE AND DEFAULT HANDLER

You can use multiple catch expressions with a try, each one with a different parameter type. Only the catch that matches its type with the argument specified in the throw statement is executed. If you use an ellipsis (...) as the parameter of catch, that handler will catch any exception no matter what the type of the throw exception is. This can be used as a default handler that catches all exceptions not caught by other handler s if it is specified at last like:

```
try {
 // code here
}
catch (int param) { cout << "int exception"; }
catch (char param) { cout << "char exception"; }
catch (...) { cout << "default exception"; }
```

In this case the last handler would catch any exception thrown with any parameter that is neither an int nor a char. After an exception has been handled the program execution resumes after the try-catch block, not after the throw statement.

EXAMPLE 14.1

In a program there is a need to enter number of shirts in integer form but the user not entering valid numbers, that will create problem when we want to multiply strings by constant numbers. Therefore use exception handling to examine each number that the user would type and handle its exception in case of an invalid number.

```
#include <iostream>
#include <iomanip>
const double PriceShirt = 0.99;
const double PricePants = 1.75;
struct TCleaningOrder
{
    int NumberOfShirts;
    int NumberOfPants;
    int NumberOfMisc;
};
```

```
void main()
{
    TCleaningOrder Order;
    double TotalPriceShirts, TotalPricePants;
    double PriceMisc, TotalPriceMisc;
    double TotalOrder;
    cout << " - Georgetown Cleaning Services -\n";
    cout << " - Customer Order Processing -\n";
    try {
       cout << "Number of\n";
       cout << "Shirts: ";
       cin >> Order.NumberOfShirts;
       if( isdigit(Order.NumberOfShirts) )
       throw Order.NumberOfShirts;
       cout << "Pairs of Paints: ";
       cin >> Order.NumberOfPants;
       if( isdigit(Order.NumberOfPants) )
          throw Order.NumberOfPants;
       cout << "Misc. Items(if none, type 0): ";
       cin >> Order.NumberMisc;
       if( isdigit(Order.NumberOfMisc) )
          throw Order.NumberOfMisc;
       if(Order.NumberMisc > 0)
    {
       cout << "Enter the price of each miscellanous item: ";
       cin >> PriceMisc;
       TotalPriceMisc = Order.NumberOfMisc * PriceMisc;
}
```

14.4 STANDARD EXCEPTIONS

The C++ Standard library provides a base class specifically designed to declare objects to be thrown as exceptions. It is called exception and is defined in the <exception.h> header file. This class has the usual default and copy constructors, operators and destructors, plus an additional virtual member function called what that returns a null-terminated character sequence (char *) and that can be redefined in derived class to contain some sort of description of the exception.

EXAMPLE 14.2

```
#include <iostream>
#include <exception>
```

```
class myexception: public exception
{
    virtual const char* what() const
    {
        return "My exception start";
    }
} myex;

void main () {
    try
    {
        throw myex;
    }
    catch (exception& e)
    {
        cout << e.what() << endl;
    }
    return 0;
}
```

All exceptions thrown by components of the C++ Standard library throw exceptions derived from this `std::exception class`. These are:

EXCEPTION	MEANING
bad_alloc	thrown by new on allocation failure
bad_cast	thrown by dynamic_cast when fails with a referenced type
bad_exception	thrown when an exception type doesn't match any catch
Bad_typeid	thrown by typeid
Ios_base::failure	thrown by functions in the iostream library

For example, if we use the operator new without (nothrow) and the memory cannot be allocated, an exception of type bad_alloc is thrown:

```
try {
    int * myarray= new int [1000];
}
catch (bad_alloc&)
{
    cout << "Error in allocating memory" << endl;
}
```

REVIEW QUESTIONS

1. What is an exception and why you should take care of exceptions in a large program?
2. What are the steps to provide exception habdling in a C++ program?
3. What is a catch statement, can you use multiple catch, if yes how?
4. What information can an exception contain, what will be the form of exception?
5. When are exception objects created?
6. Should you pass exceptions by value or by reference?
7. Will a catch statement catch a derived exception if it is looking for the base class?
8. If there are two catch statements, one for base and one for derived, which should come first?

LAB EXERCISES

1. Create a try block, a catch statement, and a simple exception to trap divide by zero exception.
2. Use number data for a character input and try to trace o the exception, along with an accessor function, and use it in the catch block.
3. Modify the class from Exercise 2 to be a hierarchy of exceptions. Modify the catch block to use the derived objects and the base objects.
4. What is wrong with the following code?

```
class OutOfMemory
{
public:
   OutOfMemory( const String& message ): itsMsg( message ){}
   ~OutOfMemory(){}
   virtual const String& Message(){ return itsMsg};
private:
   String itsMsg;
}
main()
{
   try {
      char *var = new char;
      if ( var == 0 )
         throw xOutOfMemory();
   }
   catch( OutOfMemory& theException )
   {
      cout << theException.Message() << "\n";
   }
}
```

Chapter 15 TEMPLATES

15.1 TEMPLATES

In C++, *templates* are used to define generic functions and classes. A *generic* function or class is one which takes a type as an actual parameter. As a result, a single function or class definition gives rise to a family of functions or classes that are compiled from the same source code, but operate on different types. Templates offer the preferred method of creating parameterized lists in C++. They are an integrated part of the language, they are type-safe, and they are very flexible. You are already with polymorphism in that you can overload functions to perform same task but the limitation is that you have to use different functions for different type passing. Using template you can pass multiple values even using a single function name.

EXAMPLE 15.1

Consider the following function definition:

```
int Max (int x, int y)

{ return x > y? x: y; }
```

The Max function takes to arguments of type int and returns the larger of the two. To compute the maximum value of a pair of float or doubles, we require a different Max function. By using a template, we can define a generic Max function like this:

```
template <class T>

T Max (T x, T y)

{ return x > y? x: y; }
```

The template definition gives rise to a family of Max functions, one for every different type T. The C++ compiler automatically creates the appropriate Max functions as needed. Like:

int i = Max (1, 2);

float f=Max(1.4,1.2);

double d = Max (1.0, 2.0);

Now only one template can handle the Max functions for arguments of type int, float or double.

15.2 FUNCTION TEMPLATES

Function templates are special functions that can operate with generic types. This allows us to create a functiontemplatewhose functionality can be adapted to more than one variable type or class without repeating the code for each type. This is achieved through template *parameters*. A template parameter is a special kind of parameter that can be used to pass a type as parameter. These function templates can use these parameters as if they were regular types. The format for declaring function templates with type parameters is:

```
template <class identifier> function_declaration;

template <typename identifier> function_declaration;
```

The only difference between both prototypes is the use of either the keyword class or the keyword typename. Its use is indistinct since both expressions have exactly the same meaning and behave exactly the same way. For example, to create a template function that returns the greater one of two objects you can use:

```
template <class myType>
myType GetMax (myType a, myType b) {
return (a>b?a:b);
}
```

EXAMPLE 15.2

```
// template multiply, which can be used to multiply integer, float or
double numbers
#include <iostream.h>
template <class T>
T Multiply (T a, T b) {
T result;
result = a * b;
return (result);
}
void main () {
int i=5, j=6, k;
float x=2.3, y=3.4, z;
long l=10.0, m=5.0, n;
k= Multiply <int>(i,j);
z= Multiply <float>(i,j);
n= Multiply <long>(l,m);
```

```
    cout << k << endl;
    cout<<z<<endl;
    cout << n << endl;
}
```

EXAMPLE 15.3

```
// class template
template < class T>
class sum {
T values [2];
public:
sum (T first, T second)
    {
       values[0]=first;  values[1]=second;
    }
};
```

The class that we have just defined serves to store two elements of any valid type. For example, if we wanted to declare an object of this class to store two integer values of type int with the values 112 and 34 we would write:

```
Sum <int> obj1(112,34)
```

this same class would also be used to create an object to store any other type: -

```
sum <float> obj1(3.5,6.7)
```

EXAMPLE 15.4

```
// template class to find larger number in two numbers of any type
#include <iostream>
template <class T>
class findmax {
    T a, b;
    public:
    findmax (T first, T second)
    {a=first; b=second;}
    T getmax ();
};
template <class T>
T findmax<T>::getmax ()
{
    T retval;
    retval = a>b? a:b;
    return retval;
}
```

```
    void main () {
    findmax <int> myobject (100, 75);
    cout << myobject.getmax();
    findmax <float> myobject (10.8, 17.5);
    cout << myobject.getmax();
 }
```

15.3 TEMPLATE SPECIALIZATION

If we want to define a different implementation for a template when a specific type is passed as template parameter, we can declare a specialization of that template. For example, let's suppose that we have a very simple class called container that can store one element of any type and that it has just one member function called increase, that increases its value. But we find that when it stores an element of type char it would be more convenient to have a completely different implementation with a function member uppercase, so we decide to declare a class template specialization for that type:

```
#include <iostream>
template <class T>
class container {
       T element;
    public:
       container (T arg) {element=arg;}
       T increase () {return ++element;}
    };
       template <>
       class container <char> {
       char element;
    public:
       container (T arg) {element=arg;}
       char uppercase ();
    };
template <>
char container<char>::uppercase()
{
    if ((element>='a')&&(element<='z'))
    element+='A'-'a';
    return element;
}
    void main () {
    container<int> myint (7);
    container<char> mychar ('j');
    cout << myint.increase() << endl;
    cout << mychar.uppercase() << endl;
}
```

15.4 TEMPLATES WITH MULTI FILE PROJECTS

Templates are not normal functions or classes. They are compiled on demand, meaning that the code of a template function is not compiled until an instantiation with specific template arguments is required. At that moment, when an instantiation is required, the compiler generates a function specifically for those arguments from the template. When projects grow it is usual to split the code of a program in different source code files. In these cases, the interface and implementation are generally separated. Taking a library of functions as example, the interface generally consists of declarations of the prototypes of all the functions that can be called. These are generally declared in a "header file" with a .h extension, and the implementation (the definition of these functions) is in an independent file with c++ code. Because templates are compiled when required, this forces a restriction for multi-file projects the implementation (definition) of a template class or function must be in the same file as its declaration. That means that we cannot separate the interface in a separate header file, and that we must include both interface and implementation in any file that uses the templates. Since no code is generated until a template is instantiated when required, compilers are prepared to allow the inclusion more than once of the same template file with both declarations and definitions in a project without generating linkage errors.

15.5 STANDARD TEMPLATE LIBRARY (STL)

A new development in C++ is the adoption of the Standard Template Library (STL). All the major compiler vendors now offer the STL as part of their compilers. STL is a library of template-based container classes, including vectors, lists, queues, and stacks. The STL also includes a number of common algorithms, including sorting and searching. The goal of the STL is to give you an alternative to reinventing the wheel for these common requirements. The STL is tested and debugged, offers high performance, and is free. Most important, the STL is reusable; once you understand how to use an STL container, you can use it in all your programs without reinventing it.

REVIEW QUESTIONS

1. What is the difference between a template and a macro?
2. What is the difference between polymorphism and template function?
3. What is the difference between a template class and a template function?
4. What is STL?

LAB EXERCISES

1. Write a template based program to concate two numbers, characters and strings.
2. Design a template to compute average of 10 integer, float, long values.

Chapter 16

PREPROCESSOR DERIVATIVES IN C++

16.1 PREPROCESSOR DERIVATIVES

Preprocessor directives are lines included in the code of our programs that are not program statements but directives for the preprocessor. These lines are always preceded by a pound sign (#). The preprocessor is executed before the actual compilation of code begins, therefore the preprocessor digests all these directives before any code is generated by the statements. These preprocessor directives extend only across a single line of code. As soon as a newline character is found, the preprocessor directive is considered to end. No semicolon (;) is expected at the end of a preprocessor directive. The only way a preprocessor directive can extend through more than one line is by preceding the newline character at the end of the line by a backslash (\).

16.1.1 #define

To define preprocessor macros we can use #define. Its format is: -

```
#define identifier replacement

#define TRUE 1
```

When the preprocessor encounters this directive, it replaces any occurrence of identifier in the rest of the code by replacement. This replacement can be an expression, a statement, a block or simply anything. The preprocessor does not understand C++, it simply replaces any occurrence of identifier by replacement.

```
#define TABLESIZE 100

int table1[TABLESIZE];

int table2[TABLESIZE];
```

After the preprocessor has replaced TABLE_SIZE, the code becomes equivalent to:

```
int table1[100];

int table2[100];
```

EXAMPLE 16.1

```
// Use of #define to develop a function getmin() to find minimum in
two numbers
include <iostream.h>
#define getmin(a,b)  ((a)<(b)?(a):(b))
void main()
{
    int x=5, y=8;
    y= getmin(x,y);
    cout << y << endl;
}
```

16.1.2 # And #

Function macro definitions accept two special operators (# and ##) in the replacement sequence. If the operator # is used before a parameter is used in the replacement sequence, that parameter is replaced by a string literal (as if it were enclosed between double quotes), The operator ## concatenates two arguments leaving no blank spaces between them. Like:

```
#define str(x) #x
cout << str(test);
output will be "test"

#define join(a,b) a ## b
    join(c,out)<<"test"
output will be cout<< "test"
```

16.1.3 #undef

If you have defined some value using #define you can erase it using #undef in a program. Like:

```
#define TABLESIZE 100
int table1[TABLESIZE]
#undef TABLESIZE
#define TABLESIZE 200
int table2[TABLESIZE]
```

You will get

```
table1[100]
table2[200]
```

16.2 CONDITIONAL INCLUSIONS

These directives allow to include or discard part of the code of a program if a certain condition is met. The main conditional inclusions are:

```
#ifdef, #ifndef, #if, #endif, #else and #elif
```

#ifdef allows a section of a program to be compiled only if the macro that is specified as the parameter has been defined, no matter which its value is. For example: -

```
#ifdef TABLESIZE

int table[TABLESIZE]

#endif
```

In this case, the line of code int table[TABLESIZE]; is only compiled if TABLE_SIZE was previously defined with #define, independently of its value. If it was not defined, that line will not be included in the program compilation. #ifndef serves for the exact opposite, the code between #ifndef and #endif directives is only compiled if the specified identifier has not been previously defined. For example:

```
#ifndef TABLESIZE

#define TABLESIZE 100

#endif

int table[TABLESIZE]
```

The #if, #else and #elif (i.e., "else if") directives serve to specify some condition to be met in order for the portion of code they surround to be compiled. The condition that follows #if or #elif can only evaluate constant expressions, including macro expressions. For example:

```
#if TABLE_SIZE>200
#undef TABLE_SIZE
#define TABLE_SIZE 200
#elif TABLE_SIZE<50
#undef TABLE_SIZE
#define TABLE_SIZE 50
#else
#undef TABLE_SIZE
#define TABLE_SIZE 100
#endif
int table[TABLE_SIZE];
```

16.3 #LINE

When we compile a program and some error happen during the compiling process, the compiler shows an error message with references to the name of the file where the error happened and a line number, so it is easier to find the code generating the error. The #line directive allows us to control both things, the line numbers within the code files as well as the file name that we want that appears when an error takes place. Its format is:

```
#line number "filename"
```

Where number is the new line number that will be assigned to the next code line. The line numbers of successive lines will be increased one by one from this point on.

16.4 SOURCE FILE INCLUSION DERIVATIVE

This directive has also been used assiduously in all programs of this book. When the preprocessor finds an #include directive it replaces it by the entire content of the specified file. There are two ways to specify a file to be included:

```
#include "file"     #include "iostream.h"
#include <file>     #include <math.h>
```

REVIEW QUESTIONS

1. What do you mean by preprocessor derivatives?
2. How do you use #define to set values of constants in your program?
3. What is the difference between #define debug 0 and #undef debug?
4. Name four preprocessor derivatives with examples.

LAB EXERCISES

1. Write the inclusion statements for the header file graphics.h
2. Write an merror() macro that prints an error message and the file and line number if debug level is 2, just a message (without file and line number) if the level is 1, and does nothing if the level is 0.
3. Write a macro cube to prints the cube value passed a number as a parameter.
4. Write a function that prints an error message. The function should print the line number and filename where the error occurred. Note that the line number and filename are passed in to this function.

Chapter 17

GRAPHICS PROGRAMMING IN C++

17.1 COMPUTER GRAPHICS

For a computer science students the meaning of graphics can be:

- *Graphics* implemented through the use of computers using basic shapes like lines, circles, arcs etc.
- Methods and techniques for converting *data* to or from graphic displays via computers using scanners, digital cameras, mobile handsets etc.
- The branch of science and technology concerned with methods and techniques for converting data to or from visual presentation using computers with the help of programming languages like 'C' or C++.

17.2 GRAPHICS PROGRAMMING IN C++

To start with graphics programming, C++ is a good choice. Even though other languages like BASIC, C can be used but they have their own limitations. C++ is having a large number of useful functions that can be accessed with the help of objects and is easy to program. To implement graphics algorithms like to show graphical display of statistics data using bar or pie charts or to design graphical games you can use library functions of C++ in a program. C++ has a good collection of graphics libraries.

17.3 REQUIREMENTS FOR GRAPHIC DESIGNING

To start graphics programming in C++, You need graphics.h header file, graphics.lib library file and Graphics driver (BGI file) that are stored with your C++ programs folder. These files are part of

C++ package. A color monitor to display graphics and graphics driver file like EGAVGA.BGI is also required.

17.4 BASIC SHAPES OF GRAPHICS

To start graphics design in C++, you have to be familiar with some basic shapes and function used to draw that shapes. Like:

1. Lines
2. Circle
3. Rectangle
4. Arc and many more.

And to fill colors in that shapes you can l use again some predefined functions like setcolor() or setbkcolor().

17.5 YOUR FIRST GRAPHICS PROGRAM

```
// Program to draw a circle
#include<graphics.h>
#include<conio.h>
void main()
{
    int gd=DETECT, gm;
    initgraph(&gd, &gm, " " );
    circle(200,100,150);
    getch();
    closegraph();
}
```

As you can see in the sample program

1. You must include graphics.h file, which has definations of all graphical functions.
2. Use DETECT keyword always to search the graphical driver for your monitor, on which you will get the display.
3. Use initgraph() method and pass three values, information about graphics driver, mode of graphics and path for graphics driver file.
4. Use any shape draw method like circle(), to draw the shape.
5. Close the graphocs settings using closegraph() method.

17.6 LINES DRAWING

To draw lines the function is

```
line(int x1,int y1,int x2,int y2) // x1,y1,x2,y2 are the coordinates
line(10,20,110,20) // will draw a horizontal line like ----------
```

EXAMPLE 17.1

```
#include<graphics.h>
#include<conio.h>
void main()
{
    int gd=DETECT, gm;
    initgraph(&gd, &gm, " " );
    line(100,250,540,250);
    outtextxy(300,260,"Line");
    getch();
    closegraph();
}
```

17.7 CIRCLES DRAWING

To draw a circle use the function

```
circle(int x1,int y1,redius) // where x1, y1 are center of circle
```

circle() function takes x, y coordinates as center of the circle with respect to left top of the screen and radius of the circle in terms of pixels as arguments.

```
circle(100,100,50 ) // will draw a circle of 50 radius
```

EXAMPLE 17.2

```
#include<graphics.h>
#include<conio.h>
void main()
{
    int gd=DETECT, gm;
    initgraph(&gd, &gm, " " );
    circle(100,100,50);
    outtextxy(75,170, "Circle");
    getch();
    closegraph();
}
```

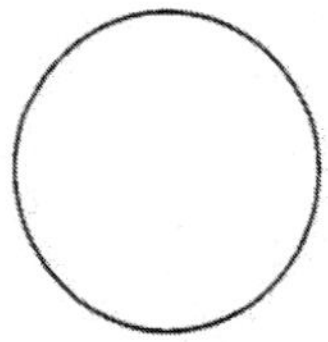

Circle

17.8 RECTANGLE DRAWING

To draw a rectangle use the function

```
rectangle(int x1,int y1,int x2,int y2)
rectangle(10,20,30,40)
```

EXAMPLE 17.3

```
#include<graphics.h>
#include<conio.h>
void main()
{
    int gd=DETECT, gm;
    initgraph(&gd, &gm, " " );
    rectangle(200,50,350,150);
    outtextxy(240, 170, "Rectangle");
    getch();
    closegraph();
 }
```

Rectangle

17.9 ELLIPSE DRAWING

To draw a ellipse use the function

```
ellipse(x1,y1,startangle,endengle,xradius,yradius)
ellipse(10,20,30,60,60,90)
```

EXAMPLE 17.4

```
void main()
{
    int gd=DETECT, gm;
    initgraph(&gd, &gm, " " );
    ellipse(500, 100,0,360, 100,50);
    getch();
    closegraph();
}
```

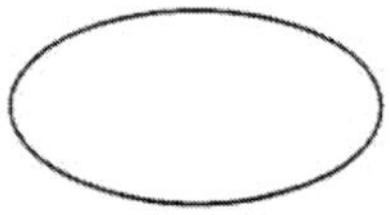

Ellipse

17.10 FILL COLORS IN SHAPES

There are 16 colors declared in graphics.h as listed bellow:

Color	Number code
BLACK	0
BLUE	1
GREEN	2
CYAN	3
RED	4
MAGENTA	5
BROWN	6
LIGHTGRAY	7
DARKGRAY	8
LIGHTBLUE	9
LIGHTGREEN	10
LIGHTCYAN	11
LIGHTRED:	12
LIGHTMAGENTA	13
YELLOW	14
WHITE	15

To use these colors, use functions

- setcolor()
- setbkcolor()
- setfillstyle()

setcolor() function sets the current drawing color. If we use setcolor(RED); and draw any shape, line or text after that, the drawing will be in red color. You can either use color as defined above or number like setcolor(4); setbkcolor() sets background color for drawing.

Setfillstyle sets fill pattern and fill colors. After calling setfillstyle, if we use functions like floodfill, fillpoly, bar etc, shapes will be filled with fill color and pattern set using setfillstyle.

EXAMPLE 17.5

```
void main()
{
    int gd=DETECT, gm;
    initgraph(&gd, &gm, " " );
    setcolor(2); //set green color
    circle(100,100,50);
    outtextxy(75,170, "Circle");
    getch();
    closegraph();
}
```

17.11 SET FILL STYLES IN SHAPES

The parameter pattern to set fill style is as follows:

Names	Value	Fill With
EMPTY_FILL	0	Background color
SOLID_FILL	1	Solid fill
LINE_FILL	2	—
LTSLASH_FILL	3	///
SLASH_FILL	4	///, thick lines
BKSLASH_FILL	5	\\\, thick lines
LTBKSLASH_FILL	6	\\\
HATCH_FILL	7	Light hatch
XHATCH_FILL	8	Heavy crosshatch
INTERLEAVE_FILL	9	Interleaving lines
WIDE_DOT_FILL	10	Widely spaced dots
CLOSE_DOT_FILL	11	Closely spaced dots
USER_FILL	12	User-defined fill pattern

EXAMPLE 17.6

```
#include "graphics.h"
#include "conio.h"
#include "stdlib.h"
void main()
{
    int gd,gm;
    gd=DETECT;
    initgraph(&gd, &gm, "");
    setcolor(3);
    setfillstyle(SOLID_FILL,4);
    bar(50, 50, 590, 430);
    setfillstyle(1, 14);
    bar(100, 100, 540, 380);
    while(!kbhit())
```

```
{
    putpixel(random(439)+101,  random(279)+101,random(16));
    setcolor(random(16));
    circle(320,240,random(100));
}
    getch();
    closegraph();
}
```

REVIEW QUESTIONS

1. Define the word computer graphics.
2. What are the basic requirements to start graphics programming in C.
3. Write the syntax to draw lines with an example.
4. Write the syntax to draw a circle with an example
5. Write the syntax to draw rectangle with an example
6. What are the common methods to fill colors in shapes?

LAB EXERCISES

1. Write program to draw horizontal line on full screen.
2. Write program to draw vertical lines on full screen.
3. Draw a grid on screen use red and green colors.
4. Draw random circles on screen in random colors.
5. Draw national flag of India.
6. Desing a smiling face on screen.
7. Draw a rectangle and then draw fill circle in it.
8. Draw a hut.
9. Draw all shapes togather in a single program.
10. Desing a graphical game of your choice.

APPENDIX-I

C++ PROJECTS

PROJECT 1: DRAW PIE / BAR CHARTS ON GIVEN VALUES

```
#include<stdio.h>
#include<stdlib.h>
#include<graphics.h>
#include<math.h>

void main()
{
  int i,n,value[10],max=0;
  int gd=DETECT,gm=CGAC0;
  int totval=0;
  char lab[20][15];

  value[0]=0;
  puts("Title of Graph ...(As:Run rate chart)");
  gets(lab[0]);
  cout<<" Total no. of values (Use number less than 8 )";
  do
```

```
   {cin>>n;} while(n>10);
   cout<<"To print graph; Type Label/Heading and values:(Integer only)";
   cout<<"\n (Eg: Over15"<<"\n Over26";
   for(i=1;i<=n;i++)
   {
     cout<<,i;
     scanf("%s%d",&lab[i],&value[i]);
     if(value[i]>max)
       max=value[i];
     totval+=value[i];
   }
   initgraph(&gd,&gm,"*.*");
   slicechart(value,n,totval,lab);
   usebar(value,n,max,lab);
   closegraph();
}
slicechart(int *array,int totno,int sum,char lable[20][15])
{
   int i=1,x,y;
   char buffer[10];
   float angle[11],xdir,ydir,totang=0;
   x=getmaxx();
   y=getmaxy();
   while(i<=totno)
{
   angle[i]= (array[i]*360.0/ sum);
   totang+=angle[i];
   setfillstyle(1,i);
   pieslice(x/2,y/2, totang-angle[i],totang,150);

   xdir=cos((totang - angle[i]/2.0) *3.14/180.0); /*to get x-y
                                                      coordinates */
   ydir=sin(( totang - angle[i]/2.0) *3.14/180.0);
   itoa(angle[i]*100/360,buffer,10); /* convrt to string */
   moveto(x/2+ xdir*170-7, y/2-ydir*170);
   outtext( buffer);
   outtext("%");
```

```
    bar(10,300+20*i,20,300+20*i+10);
    outtextxy(35,300+20*i,lable[i]);
    itoa(
    array[i],buffer,10);
    outtextxy(120,300+20*i,buffer);
    i++;
    }
    setcolor(YELLOW);
    rectangle(5,315,150,290+20*i);

    settextjustify(CENTER_TEXT,TOP_TEXT);
    settextstyle(1,0,5);
    outtextxy(x/2,5,lable[0]);
    getch();
    return;
  }
  usebar(unsigned int *array,int totno,int max,char lab[15][15])
  {
    int i;
    float length;
    char buffer[5];

    clearviewport();
    line(50,40,50,450);
    line(50,450,600,450);
    for(i=1;i<=totno;i++)
    {
    setcolor(YELLOW);
    setfillstyle(i,i);
    length=array[i]*400/max;
    bar3d(i*70,450-length,50+i*70,450,10,10);
    itoa(array[i],buffer,10);
    settextstyle(2,0,8);
    setcolor(WHITE);
    outtextxy(i*70+25,420-length,buffer);

    settextstyle(2,0,5);
    outtextxy(i*70+25,455,lab[i]);
    }
```

```
for(i=0;i<=10;i++)
{
  moveto(40,40*i+50);
  settextjustify(RIGHT_TEXT,BOTTOM_TEXT);
  itoa(max*(10-i)/10,buffer,10);
  outtext(buffer);
  lineto(50,40*i+50);

}
getch();
return;
}
```

PROJECT 2: SIMPLE GRAPHICS DESIGN (a)

```
/*simple graphics project -Mk sharma*/
#include<stdio.h>
#include<stdlib.h>
#include<conio.h>
#include <graphics.h>
main()
{

  int x1=600;
  int gd=DETECT,gm=EGAHI;
  initgraph(&gd,&gm,"");

  clrscr();


  for(;;x1++)
  {
    x1%=250;
    setcolor(random(16));

    circle(random(635),random(470),50);
    circle(random(635),random(470),50);
    circle(random(635),random(470),50);
```

```
    circle(random(635),random(470),50);
    circle(random(635),random(470),50);

   clearviewport();
   settextstyle(1,0,5);
   setcolor(RED);
   outtextxy(89,415-2*x1, "* MK SHARMA *");
   setcolor(random(16));
   outtextxy (109,315-2*x1, "* KS VAISLA *");
   setcolor(GREEN);
   settextstyle(3,0,5);
   outtextxy(70,655-2*x1,"AMRAPALI  INSTITUTE");

  if(kbhit())
    break;
  }
  closegraph();
```

Simple Graphics design (b)

```
#include<stdio.h>
#include<stdlib.h>
#include<conio.h>
#include <graphics.h>
main()
{
 int x1=600,y1=1,x2=100,y2=100;
 int shape=1,ranc=1,ranp;
 int gd=DETECT,gm;
 initgraph(&gd,&gm,"");

 cleardevice();


 for(;;x1++)
 {
 if(x1>=250)
 {
```

```
    ranc=random(600);
    x1=0;
    x2=0;
    y1=getmaxx();
    y2=getmaxy();
    shape=(shape+1) %3;
 }

 setcolor(ranc%16);
 switch(shape)
 {
  case 0:
    rectangle(x1,x2,y1,y2);
   break;
  case 1:
    circle(320,240,y2/2);
   break;
  case 2:
    circle(100,100,y2/4);
    circle(100,370,y2/4);
    circle(530,100,y2/4);
    circle(530,370,y2/4);
  }
  setcolor(random(16) );
  outtextxy(103,217,"* MK SHARMA *");
  outtextxy(random(640),random(480),".");
  setcolor(BLACK);
  settextstyle(1,0,5);
  outtextxy(103,315,"* VANDANA SHARMA *");
 x2++;
 y1--;
 y2--;

 /* delay(1000);*/

 if(kbhit())
 break;
 }
```

```
 closegraph();

 return;
}

Simple Graphics design (c)

/*simple graphics effects
 MKSHARMA & KS VAISLA
*/

#include<stdio.h>
#include<stdlib.h>
#include<graphics.h>

main()
{
 int i,col=1,x,y;
 int gd=DETECT,gm=CGAC0;


  initgraph(&gd,&gm,"");
  clearviewport();
  setcolor(YELLOW);
  setwritemode(1);
  rectangle(250,200,350,300);
 do
 {
 col%=51;

  setcolor(RED);
  rectangle(250+col,200+col,350-col,300-col);
 outtextxy(250,350,"Hello World !");
 delay(40);
 col+=2;
 }while(!kbhit());

 getch();
```

```
  closegraph();
  return;

}
```

PROJECT 3: TIC - TAC - TOE GAME

```
#include<stdio.h>
#include<conio.h>
#include<stdlib.h>
#include<graphics.h>

int board[10], turn = 1, flag = 0, player, comp;
int x1 = 220, y1 = 70, x2 = 230, y2 = 130;
int key, cp = 1, cx = 0, cy = 0;
enum { up = 72, left = 75, right = 77, down = 80} direction;
enum { yes , no } selected;

void menu();
void reset();
void go(int n);
void start_game();
void check_draw();
void draw_board();
void take_input();
void status_bar();
void player_first();
void put_X_O(char *ch,int pos);
void user_choice(int ycolor,int ncolor,char *str1,char *str2);

void main()
{
  int gd = DETECT, gm;

  initgraph(&gd,&gm,"c:\\tc\\bgi");
  reset();
  menu();
```

```
  getch();
}

void reset()
{
  int i;
  for(i=1;i<10;i++)
    board[i] = 2;
  turn = 1;
  flag = 0;
  x1 = 170, y1 = 70, x2 = 230, y2 = 130;
}


void menu()
{
  cleardevice();
  if(yesno(0))
  {
    player = 0;
    comp = 1;
    cleardevice();
    start_game();
  }
  else
  {
    player = 1;
    comp = 0;
    cleardevice();
    player_first();
  }
}

int make2()
{
  if(board[5] == 2)
    return 5;
  if(board[2] == 2)
    return 2;
```

```
  if(board[4] == 2)
    return 4;
  if(board[6] == 2)
    return 6;
  if(board[8] == 2)
    return 8;
  return 0;
}

int make4()
{
  if(board[1] == 2)
    return 1;
  if(board[3] == 2)
    return 3;
  if(board[7] == 2)
    return 7;
  if(board[9] == 2)
    return 9;
  return 0;
}

int posswin(int p)
{
// p==1 then X p==0 then O
  int i;
  int check_val,pos;

  if(p == 1)
    check_val = 18;
  else
    check_val = 50;

  i = 1;
  while(i<=9)//row check
  {
    if(board[i] * board[i+1] * board[i+2] == check_val)
```

```
    {
      if(board[i] == 2)
        return i;
      if(board[i+1] == 2)
        return i+1;
      if(board[i+2] == 2)
        return i+2;
    }
    i+=3;
  }

  i = 1;
  while(i<=3)//column check
  {
    if(board[i] * board[i+3] * board[i+6] == check_val)
    {
      if(board[i] == 2)
        return i;
      if(board[i+3] == 2)
        return i+3;
      if(board[i+6] == 2)
        return i+6;
    }
    i++;
  }

  if(board[1] * board[5] * board[9] == check_val)
  {
    if(board[1] == 2)
      return 1;
    if(board[5] == 2)
      return 5;
    if(board[9] == 2)
      return 9;
  }

  if(board[3] * board[5] * board[7] == check_val)
```

```
  {
    if(board[3] == 2)
      return 3;
    if(board[5] == 2)
      return 5;
    if(board[7] == 2)
      return 7;
  }
  return 0;
}

void go(int n)
{
  if(turn % 2)
    board[n] = 3;
  else
    board[n] = 5;
  turn++;
}

void player_first()
{
  check_draw();
  draw_board();
  status_bar();
  take_input();
}

void start_game()
{
  // p==1 then X p==0 then O
  if(posswin(comp))
  {
    go(posswin(comp));
    flag = 1;
  }
  else
  if(posswin(player))
```

```
    go(posswin(player));
  else
  if(make2())
    go(make2());
  else
    go(make4());
  draw_board();

  if(flag)
  {
    settextstyle(1,0,4);
    settextjustify(1,1);
    setcolor(128+RED);
    outtextxy(320,380,"Computer  wins");
    getch();
    exit(0);
  }
  else
    player_first();
}

void check_draw()
{
  if(turn > 9)
  {
    settextstyle(1,0,4);
    settextjustify(1,1);
    setcolor(128+RED);
    outtextxy(320,380,"Game  Draw");
    getch();
    exit(0);
  }
}

void put_X_O(char *ch,int pos)
{
  int m;
  int x = 170, y = 70;
```

```
  m = pos;
  if(m > 3)
  {
    while(m > 3)
    {
      y += 100;
      m -= 3;
    }
  }
  if(pos % 3 == 0)
    x += 200;
  else
  {
    pos %= 3;
    pos--;
    while(pos)
    {
      x += 100;
      pos--;
    }
  }
  settextstyle(1,0,7);
  settextjustify(1,1);
  setcolor(9);
  outtextxy(x+30,y+20,ch);
}

void draw_board()
{
  int j;

  setfillstyle(1,3);
  bar(150,50,450,350);
  setlinestyle(0,0,3);
  setcolor(4);
  rectangle(148,48,452,352);
  line(250,50,250,350);
  line(350,50,350,350);
```

```
    line(150,150,450,150);
    line(150,250,450,250);
    setcolor(9);
    rectangle(x1,y1,x2,y2);

    for(j=1;j<10;j++)
    {
      if(board[j] == 3)
        put_X_O("X",j);
      else
      if(board[j] == 5)
        put_X_O("O",j);
    }
}

void take_input()
{
    status_bar();
    while(1)
    {
      if(kbhit())
      {
        flushall();
        key = getch();
        //if status bar invoked
        switch (key)
        {
          case 13:
          if(board[cp] != 2)
            break;
          if(cp == posswin(player))
          {
            go(cp);
            draw_board();
            settextstyle(1,0,4);
            settextjustify(1,1);
            setcolor(128+RED);
            outtextxy(320,380,"Player Wins");
```

```
    getch();
    exit(0);
  }
  go(cp);
  draw_board();
  start_game();
  break;
  case 32:
    settextstyle(1,0,4);
    settextjustify(1,1);
    setcolor(128+BLUE);
    outtextxy(320,240,"Press Space bar to continue...");
    while(getch() != 32)
      continue;
    setcolor(0);
    outtextxy(320,240,"Press Space bar to continue...");
    draw_board();
    break;
  case 78:
  case 110:
    if(yesno(1))
    {
      cp = 1;
      cx = 0;
      cy = 0;
      reset();
      main();
    }
    cleardevice();
    draw_board();
    status_bar();
    break;
  case 88:
  case 120:
    if(yesno(1))
      exit(0);
    cleardevice();
    status_bar();
```

```
        draw_board();
        break;
      case up:
        if(cx > 0 )
        {
          setcolor(3);
          rectangle(x1,y1,x2,y2);
          setcolor(9);
          rectangle(x1,y1-100,x2,y2-100);
          y1=y1-100;
          y2=y2-100;
          cx=cx-1;
          cp=cp-3;
        }
        break;
      case down:
        if(cx < 2 )
        {
          setcolor(3);
          rectangle(x1,y1,x2,y2);
          setcolor(9);
          rectangle(x1,y1+100,x2,y2+100);
          y1=y1+100;
          y2=y2+100;
          cx=cx+1;
          cp=cp+3;
        }
        break;
      case left:
        if(cy > 0 )
        {
          setcolor(3);
          rectangle(x1,y1,x2,y2);
          setcolor(9);
          rectangle(x1-100,y1,x2-100,y2);
          x1=x1-100;
          x2=x2-100;
          cy=cy-1;
```

```
            cp=cp-1;
          }
          break;
        case right:
          if(cy < 2 )
          {
            setcolor(3);
            rectangle(x1,y1,x2,y2);
            setcolor(9);
            rectangle(x1+100,y1,x2+100,y2);
            x1=x1+100;
            x2=x2+100;
            cy=cy+1;
            cp=cp+1;
          }
          break;
      }
    }
  }
}

int yesno(int choice)
{
  int user_key;
  char *s1, *s2, *s3;
  selected = no;
  settextstyle(1,0,4);
  settextjustify(1,1);
  setcolor(128+BLUE);
  if(choice)
  {
    s1 = "Are you sure ?";
    s2 = "YES";
    s3 = "NO";
  }
  else
  {
    s1 = "Select your Symbol";
```

```
    s2 = "O";
    s3 = "X";
  }
  outtextxy(320,200,s1);
  user_choice(0,2,s2,s3);

  while(1)
  {
    user_key = getch();
    switch(user_key)
    {
      case 75:
      case 77:
        if(selected == no)
        {
          user_choice(2,0,s2,s3);
          selected=yes;
        }
        else
        {
          user_choice(0,2,s2,s3);
          selected=no;
        }
        break;
      case 13:
        if(selected == yes)
          return 1;
        return 0;
    }
  }
}

void user_choice(int ycolor,int ncolor,char *str1,char *str2)
{
  setfillstyle(1,ycolor);
  bar(215,240,305,280);
  outtextxy(260,260,str1);
  setfillstyle(1,ncolor);
```

```
  bar(335,240,425,280);
  outtextxy(380,260,str2);
}


void status_bar()
{
  setfillstyle(1,BLUE);
  bar(95,430,490,460);
  setcolor(GREEN);
  settextstyle(1,0,3);
  settextjustify(0,0);
  outtextxy(100,450,"N: New");
  outtextxy(220,450,"Space: Pause");
  outtextxy(400,450,"X: Exit");
  setlinestyle(0,1,4);
}
```

Project 4: Snake Game

```
#include<dir.h>
#include<stdlib.h>
#include<stdio.h>
#include<graphics.h>
#include<conio.h>
#include<math.h>
#include<dos.h>
#include<stdio.h>
#include<process.h>
#include<graphics.h>
#include<errno.h>

int touchscreen();
int touchsnakebody();
void rightcode();
void leftcode();
void upcode();
```

```
void downcode();
void continuecode();
void ifeat();
void graphicsprinttarget();
void getgraphics();
void graphics1();
void graphicsprintsnake();
void showscore();
void reset();
void info();
void exit2();
void selectlevel();
void setkey();
int checkvalid(char);
/* Function below is not a part of actual program,
 but it is required in order to run application painlessly
*/
char *current_directory(char *path)
{
 strcpy(path, "X:\\"); /* fill string with form of response: X:\ */
 path[0] = 'A' + getdisk(); /* replace X with current drive letter */
 getcurdir(0, path+3); /* fill rest of string with current directory
*/
 return(path);
}


struct snakebody
{
 int locx,locy;
 int dir;
 };
struct target
{ int locx;
 int locy;
};

struct snakebody a[300]={0,0,0};
char ch;
```

```
struct target tar={66,66};//initialise target
int first=1;
int last=24;
int points=0,level=1,del=100;
int xt=100,yt=68;
char stringp[20],stringl[20],up[5]="w",down[5]="s",right[5]="d",
left[5]="a"; char exit3[5]="e",pause[5]="p"; //global variables


void main()
{ char try1='n';
 int gd=DETECT,gm;
 char curdir[MAXPATH];
 current_directory(curdir); //to get path of current directory
 strcat(curdir,"\\BGI");
 initgraph(&gd,&gm,curdir);
 info();

 start:

 reset();
 setkey();
 selectlevel();
 info();
 graphics1(); //initialise graphics


 a[1].locx=48;
 a[1].locy=60;
 a[1].dir=1;
 a[2].locx=42;
 a[2].locy=60;
 a[2].dir=1;
 a[3].locx=36;
 a[3].locy=60;
 a[3].dir=1;
 a[4].locx=30;
 a[4].locy=60;
 a[4].dir=1;
```

```
setcolor(RED);
settextstyle(0,0,0);
outtextxy((a[1].locx),(a[1].locy),"*");
outtextxy((a[2].locx),(a[2].locy),"*");
outtextxy((a[3].locx),(a[3].locy),"*");
outtextxy((a[4].locx),(a[4].locy),"*");//for entry point of snake
graphicsprinttarget();
while(1)
{
if(touchsnakebody())
{
settextstyle(0,0,2);
setcolor(YELLOW);
outtextxy(210,200,"Retry Y / N ?");
e2:
try1=getch();
 if((try1=='y')||(try1=='n'))
{
 if(try1=='y')
 goto start;
 else
 exit2();
}
else
goto e2;

}

 if(touchscreen() )
 { settextstyle(0,0,2);
 setcolor(YELLOW);
 outtextxy(210,200,"Retry Y / N ?");
 e1:
 try1=getch();
  if((try1=='y')||(try1=='n'))
 {
  if(try1=='y')
  goto start;
```

```
 else
 exit2();
}
else
goto e1;

}
ifeat();
if(kbhit())
{
ch=getch();
if(ch==right[0]||ch==77) {rightcode();}
if(ch==left[0] ||ch==75) {leftcode();}
if(ch==up[0] ||ch==72) {upcode();}
if(ch==down[0] ||ch==80) {downcode();}
if(ch==pause[0]){
   settextstyle(0,0,2);//for pause
   setcolor(YELLOW);
   outtextxy(140,200,"Press anykey to continue");
   getch();
   setcolor(BLUE);
   outtextxy(140,200,"Press anykey to continue");//disable previous
statement by printing same by background color

  }
 if(ch==exit3[0])exit2(1);//to exit directly from program
 }

 continuecode();
 delay(del);
 }
} /*end of main*/



int touchscreen()
{
```

```
  int i;
  if((a[first].locx <24)||(a[first].locx>=(636-24))
                       ||(a[first].locy<54)||(a[first].locy>=472))
  { graphicsprintsnake();
  settextstyle(0,0,2);
  setcolor(RED+WHITE);
  outtextxy(230,150,"Game Over");
  return (1);
  }
  return(0);
 }

 int touchsnakebody()
 {
  int i;
  //checks wheather snake face toches with any other body element
  for(i=first+1;i<=last;i++)
 {

  if((a[first].locx ==a[i].locx)&&(a[first].locy==a[i].locy))
  {
  settextstyle(0,0,2);
  setcolor(RED+WHITE);
  outtextxy(230,150,"Game Over");
  return (1);
  }
 }
 return (0);
 }

 void rightcode()
 { //changes direction variable of snake face
  if((a[first].dir !=3))
  {
  a[first].dir=1;
  }

 }
```

```
void leftcode()
{
 if((a[first].dir !=1))
 {
 a[first].dir=3;
 }

}

void upcode()
{
 if((a[first].dir!=2))
 {
 a[first].dir=4;
 }

}

void downcode()
{
 if((a[first].dir!=4))
 {
 a[first].dir=2;
 }

}

void continuecode()
{
 int i;
 graphicsprintsnake();
 for(i=last;i>=first+1;i--)
 //body elements except snake face copies the
 //direction and location variables from its precedent
 {
 a[i]=a[i-1];
 }
```

```
if(a[first].dir==1)
 a[first].locx=a[first].locx+6;
if(a[first].dir==2)
 a[first].locy+=6;
if(a[first].dir==3)
 a[first].locx-=6;
if(a[first].dir==4)
 a[first].locy-=6;

graphicsprinttarget();

}

void ifeat()
{//if target is eaten by snake increment takes place in snake length
 //& sets new target
 if((a[first].locx==tar.locx) && (a[first].locy==tar.locy))
 {last++;
 a[last]=a[last-1];//copies previous end
 randomize();
 tar.locx= random(xt)*6+54; //sets new target
 tar.locy= random(yt)*6+54;
 points++;
 if((points%5)==0)
 {
 if(level!=6)//because after level 7 delay become -ve
 { level++; //speed of snake remain 0
  del=del-20;
 }
 }
 }
 showscore();
}

void graphicsprinttarget()
{ setcolor(WHITE);
  outtextxy((tar.locx),(tar.locy),"*");
}
```

```
void graphics1()
{
 clrscr();
 clearviewport();
 settextstyle(2,0,2);
 setcolor(RED+WHITE);
 outtextxy(285,2,"Sachin");

 settextstyle(0,0,2);
 setcolor(YELLOW);
 outtextxy(260,10,"SNAKE");
 setcolor(WHITE);
 outtextxy(500,25,"score");
 outtextxy(400,25,"level");
 setcolor(YELLOW);
 rectangle(23,54,(636-23),475);
 setbkcolor(BLUE);

}

void graphicsprintsnake()
{
 settextstyle(0,0,0);
 setcolor(BLUE);
 outtextxy((a[last].locx),(a[last].locy),"*");
 setcolor(RED);
 outtextxy((a[first].locx),(a[first].locy),"*");
 }


void showscore()
{

 setcolor(BLUE);
 settextstyle(0,0,2);
 itoa( (points-1),stringp,10);
 outtextxy(530,10,stringp);//disables previous score from screen
 setcolor(WHITE);
```

```
 settextstyle(0,0,2);
 itoa(points,stringp,10);
 outtextxy(530,10,stringp);//shows score

 //shows level
 setcolor(BLUE);
 settextstyle(0,0,2);
 itoa( level-1,stringl,10);
 outtextxy(430,10,stringl);//disables previous level from screen
 setcolor(WHITE);
 settextstyle(0,0,2);
 itoa(level,stringl,10);
 outtextxy(430,10,stringl);//shows level
 }

void reset()
{//resets all global variable for restarting the game
 int j;
 first=1;
 last=24;
 points=0,level=1,del=100;
 xt=46,yt=34;
 for(j=0;j<=300;j++)
 { a[j].locx=0;
 a[j].locy=0;
 }

 tar.locx=66;
 tar.locy=66;

}

void info()
{
 clrscr();
 clearviewport();
 settextstyle(0,0,2);
 setcolor(YELLOW);
```

```
 outtextxy(230,70, "SNAKE");
 setcolor(RED+WHITE);
 outtextxy(230,110," Keys");
 outtextxy(230,150," UP "); outtextxy(340,150, up);
 outtextxy(230,190," DOWN"); outtextxy(340,190,down);
 outtextxy(230,230," RIGHT"); outtextxy(340,230,right);
 outtextxy(230,270," LEFT"); outtextxy(340,270,left);
 outtextxy(230,310," Pause"); outtextxy(340,310,pause);
 outtextxy(230,350," Exit"); outtextxy(340,350,exit3);
 outtextxy(100,400,"Press any key to continue");
 getch();
}

void exit2()
{
 closegraph();
 restorecrtmode();
 exit(1);

}

void selectlevel()
{
 char charlevel[1],option;
 int intlevel;
 clrscr();
 clearviewport();
 setbkcolor(BLUE);
 settextstyle(0,0,2);
 setcolor(YELLOW);
 outtextxy(90,200,"Do you want to set level Y/N ?");
 s1:
 option=getch();
 if((option=='y')||(option=='n'))//if 1
 {
 if(option=='y')//if 2
 {
 clearviewport();
```

```
setcolor(YELLOW);
outtextxy(100,200,"Select level between 1 to 6");
s2:
charlevel[0]=getch();
intlevel=atoi(charlevel);
 if((intlevel<1)||(intlevel>6)) //if 3
{
  goto s2;
 }//end if 3
else
{ //else 3
  level=intlevel;
  del=100-(level-1)*20;
} //end else 3


}//end if 2
}//end if 1
else
{ //else 1
goto s1;
} //end else 1

}

void setkey()
{
 char up1,down1,right1,left1,pause1,exit1,option;
 clrscr();
 clearviewport();
 settextstyle(0,0,2);
 setcolor(YELLOW);
 outtextxy(90,200,"Do you want to set keys Y/N ?");
 k1:
 option=getch();
 if((option=='y')||(option=='n'))
 { //if 1
 if(option=='y')
```

```
{//if 2
clearviewport();


while(1)
{clearviewport();
outtextxy(90,200,"Enter only character key");
outtextxy(90,240,"Enter up key");
up1=getch();
if(checkvalid(up1))
break;
}
while(1)
{clearviewport();
outtextxy(90,200,"Enter down key");
down1=getch();
if(checkvalid(down1)&&(down1!=up1))
break;
}
while(1)
{clearviewport();
outtextxy(90,200,"Enter right key");
right1=getch();
if(checkvalid(right1)&&(right1!=up1)&&(right1!=down1))
break;
}

while(1)
{clearviewport();
outtextxy(90,200,"Enter left key");
left1=getch();
if(checkvalid(left1)&&(left1!=up1)&&(left1!=down1)&&(left1!=right1))
break;
}

while(1)
{clearviewport();
outtextxy(90,200,"Enter pause key");
```

```
pause1=getch();
if(checkvalid(pause1)&&(pause1!=up1)&&(pause1!=down1)&&(pause1!=right1)
&&(pause1!=left1))
break;
}

while(1)
{clearviewport();
outtextxy(90,200,"Enter exit key");
exit1=getch();
if(checkvalid(exit1)&&(exit1!=up1)&&(exit1!=down1)&&(exit1!=right1)
&&(exit1!=left1)&&(exit1!=pause1))
break;
}
up[0]=up1;
down[0]=down1;
right[0]=right1;
left[0]=left1;
pause[0]=pause1;
exit3[0]=exit1;

}//end if2
}//end if 1
else
goto k1;
}

int checkvalid(char ke)
{
 if((ke=='a')||  (ke=='b')||(ke=='c')||(ke=='d')||(ke=='e')||
 (ke=='f')||  (ke=='g')||(ke=='h')||(ke=='i')||(ke=='j')||
 (ke=='k')||  (ke=='l')||(ke=='m')||(ke=='n')||(ke=='o')||
 (ke=='p')||  (ke=='q')||(ke=='r')||(ke=='s')||(ke=='t')||
 (ke=='u')||  (ke=='v')||(ke=='w')||(ke=='x')||(ke=='y')||
 (ke=='z'))

return(1);
else
return(0);
}
```

PROJECT 4: SNAKE & LADDER

```
#include<graphics.h>
#include<stdlib.h>
#include<stdio.h>
#include<conio.h>
#include<dos.h>
#define ESC_KEY 27


void display(int pawn[],int val)
{

 setcolor(val);
 setfillstyle(1,val);
 drawpoly(4,pawn);
 fillpoly(4,pawn);
 line(pawn[6],pawn[7],pawn[0],pawn[1]);

}

void check1(int pawn[],int val)
{
 switch(val)
 {
  case 1:
   pawn[0]=590;
   pawn[2]=600;
   pawn[4]=600;
   pawn[6]=590;
   break;

  case 2:
   pawn[0]=620;
   pawn[2]=630;
   pawn[4]=630;
   pawn[6]=620;
   break;
 }
```

```
}

void check2(int pawn[],int val)
{
 switch(val)
 {
  case 1:
   pawn[0]=10;
   pawn[2]=20;
   pawn[4]=20;
   pawn[6]=10;
   break;

  case 2:
   pawn[0]=40;
   pawn[2]=50;
   pawn[4]=50;
   pawn[6]=40;
   break;
 }

}

void Snake()
{
 /*Snake 3*/
 arc(130, 370,110,190,50);
 arc(130, 380,180,270,50);
 arc(130, 450,200,90,20);

 /*Snake 2*/
 arc(528, 180,90,260,50);
 arc(510, 280,270,80,50);
 arc(500, 390,80,185,60);

 /*Snake 1*/
 arc(108, 80,260,90,50);
 arc(90, 180,80,260,50);
```

```
 arc(75, 270,0,80,40);

}

void disp_Struct(int pawn1[],int pawn2[],char *a[],int val)
{

 int i,j,k,count=1,l;
 char msg[20];
 setcolor(11);
 setbkcolor(1);
 for(i=0;i<=640;i+=64)
    line(i,0,i,480);
 for(j=0;j<=480;j+=48)
    line(0,j,640,j);
 k=456;j=0;
 while(k>=24)
 {
  while(j<=100)
  {
    if(count%2!=0)
    {
      for(i=32,l=j;i<=608,l<=j+10;i+=64,l++)
      {
        moveto(i,k);
        outtext(a[l]);


      }
    j+=10;
    }
    else
    {
      for(i=608,l=j;i>=32,l<=j+10;i-=64,l++)
      {
        moveto(i,k);
        outtext(a[l]);
      }
```

```
        j+=10;
      }
      k-=48;
      count++;
    }
   }

   //cout<<"%d",val);
   rectangle(0,0,128,15);
   scout<<msg,"Dice value: %d",val);
   outtextxy(5,5,msg);

   display(pawn1,6);
   display(pawn2,14);

   setlinestyle(3,2,3);

   setcolor(14);
   /*Ladder 1*/
   line(234,350,406,226);
   line(220,345,392,221);

   /*Ladder 2*/
   line(460,60,540,28);
   line(485,60,565,28);

   /*Ladder 3*/
   line(210,34,410,160);
   line(235,32,435,158);

   setcolor(4);
   setlinestyle(2,1,4);
   Snake();

   setlinestyle(0,0,0);

  }
```

```
void Init_Screen()
{

 setbkcolor(0);
 setcolor(4);

 settextstyle(GOTHIC_FONT,0,6);
 outtextxy(35,22,"SNAKE AND LADDER");
 settextstyle(0,0,1);

 outtextxy(140,240,"This game is a small project");
 outtextxy(140,260,"for snakes and ladders.");
 outtextxy(160,460,"Press any key to continue.......");

 getch();
 cleardevice();

 settextstyle(GOTHIC_FONT,0,5);
 outtextxy(160,50,"CONTROLS");
 outtextxy(180,240,"SETUP");

 settextstyle(1,0,1);

 outtextxy(120,140,"Roll the Dice ........... <Enter>");
 outtextxy(120,180,"Quit the Game ........... <Esc>");

 outtextxy(120,320,"Brown Pawn ....... Player1");
 outtextxy(120,360,"Yellow Pawn ....... Computer");

 settextstyle(0,0,1);
 outtextxy(140,460,"Press any key to start the game.......");

}

void init_Disp(int pawn[],int pawn2[])
{
 pawn[0]=10;pawn[1]=458;
 pawn[2]=20;pawn[3]=458;
```

```
 pawn[4]=20;pawn[5]=448;
 pawn[6]=10;pawn[7]=448;

 pawn2[0]=40;pawn2[1]=458;
 pawn2[2]=50;pawn2[3]=458;
 pawn2[4]=50;pawn2[5]=448;
 pawn2[6]=40;pawn2[7]=448;

}

void Ladder1_func(int pawn[],int val)
{
 int i,j;
 for(j=1;j<=7;j+=2)
  pawn[j]-=144;
 check1(pawn,val);
 for(i=0;i<7;i+=2)
  pawn[i]-=192;

}

void Ladder2_func(int pawn[],int val)
{
 int i,j;
 for(j=1;j<=7;j+=2)
  pawn[j]-=144;
 check2(pawn,val);
 for(i=0;i<7;i+=2)
  pawn[i]+=192;

}

void Ladder3_func(int pawn[],int val)
{
 int i,j;
 for(j=1;j<=7;j+=2)
  pawn[j]-=48;
 check1(pawn,val);
```

```
 for(i=0;i<7;i+=2)
  pawn[i]-=64;

}

void Snake1_func(int pawn[])
{

 int i,j;
 for(j=1;j<=7;j+=2)
  pawn[j]+=240;

}

void Snake2_func(int pawn[],int val)
{
 int i,j;
 for(j=1;j<=7;j+=2)
  pawn[j]+=288;
 check1(pawn,val);
 for(i=0;i<7;i+=2)
  pawn[i]-=192;

}

void Snake3_func(int pawn[])
{
 int i,j;
 for(j=1;j<=7;j+=2)
  pawn[j]+=144;

}

void Ladder_Snake_func(int *val,int pawn[],int ct)
{
  switch(*val)
  {
```

```
    case 24:
        Ladder1_func(pawn,ct);
        *val=54;
        break;
    case 67:
        Ladder2_func(pawn,ct);
        *val=97;
        break;
    case 88:
        Ladder3_func(pawn,ct);
        *val=92;
        break;
    case 99:
        Snake1_func(pawn);
        *val=40;
        break;
    case 72:
        Snake2_func(pawn,ct);
        *val=14;
        break;
    case 39:
        Snake3_func(pawn);
        *val=2;
        break;

  }
}

void Winner_screen(int win)
{

  cleardevice();
  setbkcolor(0);
  setcolor(11);
  settextstyle(GOTHIC_FONT,0,4);

  if(win==1)
```

```
 {
  outtextxy(160,150,"WINNER IS PLAYER1");
  outtextxy(150,185,"CONGRATULATIONS............");
 }

 else
 {
  outtextxy(160,150,"WINNER IS PLAYER2");
  outtextxy(150,185,"CONGRATULATIONS............");
 }

}

int Check_for_100(int pos,int val)
{

  if((pos+val)==100)
    return 1;
  if((pos+val)>100)
    return 0;
  else
    return val;

}

void main()
{
 /* request auto detection */
 int gdriver = DETECT, gmode, errorcode;
 int pawn[8],pawn2[8];
 int i,j,k,val,cj;
 int ch1,ch,count;
 int cg1,cg,count2;
 int fg,fk,win;

 char *a[]= {"1","2","3","4","5","6","7","8","9","10",
   "11","12","13","14","15","16","17","18","19"},"20",
   "21","22","23","24","25","26","27","28","29","30",
```

```
  "31","32","33","34","35","36","37","38","39","40",
  "41","42","43","44","45","46","47","48","49","50",
  "51","52","53","54","55","56","57","58","59","60",
  "61","62","63","64","65","66","67","68","69","70",
  "71","72","73","74","75","76","77","78","79","80",
  "81","82","83","84","85","86","87","88","89","90",
  "91","92","93","94","95","96","97","98","99","100"};

clrscr();

/* initialize graphics and local variables */
initgraph(&gdriver, &gmode, "");
/* read result of initialization */
errorcode = graphresult();
/* an error occurred */
if (errorcode != grOk)
{
cout<<"Graphics error: %s\n", grapherrormsg(errorcode));
cout<<"Press any key to halt:");
getch();
exit(1); /* terminate with an error code */
}

Init_Screen();
getch();
cleardevice();
setbkcolor(0);

 init_Disp(pawn,pawn2);
 disp_Struct(pawn,pawn2,a,0);

ch=ch1=1;
cg=cg1=1;
k=1;

while(1)
{

 delay(800);
```

```
if(k%2)
{
  cj=getch();
  if(cj==ESC_KEY)
    exit(1);

  randomize();
  /*val=rand()%7;*/
  val=random(7);

  if(!val)
    val++;

  if(ch1>=94)
  {
    fg=Check_for_100(ch1,val);
    if(fg==1)
    {
      Winner_screen(1);
      getch();
      closegraph();
      exit(1);
    }
    else
      val=fg;
  }

  ch+=val;
  ch1+=val;
  count=ch1/10;

  if(ch<10&&(count%2==0))
    for(i=0;i<7;i+=2)
      pawn[i]+=val*64;

  if(ch<10&&(count%2==1))
    for(i=0;i<7;i+=2)
      pawn[i]-=val*64;
```

```
    if(ch==10&&(count%2==0))
      for(i=0;i<7;i+=2)
        pawn[i]-=val*64;

    if(ch==10&&(count%2==1))
      for(i=0;i<7;i+=2)
        pawn[i]+=val*64;

    if(ch>10&&(count%2==0))
    {
      ch=ch%10;
      check2(pawn,1);
      for(j=1;j<=7;j+=2)
        pawn[j]-=48;
      for(i=0;i<7;i+=2)
        pawn[i]+=(ch-1)*64;

    }

    if(ch>10&&(count%2==1))
    {
      ch=ch%10;
      check1(pawn,1);
      for(j=1;j<=7;j+=2)
        pawn[j]-=48;
      for(i=0;i<7;i+=2)
        pawn[i]-=(ch-1)*64;
    }

  }

  else
  {
    randomize();
    val=rand()%7;

    if(!val)
      val++;
```

```
if(cg1>=94)
{
  fk=Check_for_100(cg1,val);
  if(fk==1)
  {
    Winner_screen(2);
    getch();
    closegraph();
    exit(1);
  }
  else
    val=fk;
}

cg+=val;
cg1+=val;
count2=cg1/10;

if(cg<10&&(count2%2==0))
  for(i=0;i<7;i+=2)
    pawn2[i]+=val*64;

if(cg<10&&(count2%2==1))
  for(i=0;i<7;i+=2)
    pawn2[i]-=val*64;

if(cg==10&&(count2%2==0))
  for(i=0;i<7;i+=2)
    pawn2[i]-=val*64;

if(cg==10&&(count2%2==1))
  for(i=0;i<7;i+=2)
    pawn2[i]+=val*64;

if(cg>10&&(count2%2==0))
{
  cg=cg%10;
  check2(pawn2,2);
  for(j=1;j<=7;j+=2)
    pawn2[j]-=48;
  for(i=0;i<7;i+=2)
```

```
        pawn2[i]+=(cg-1)*64;
    }

    if(cg>10&&(count2%2==1))
    {
      cg=cg%10;
      check1(pawn2,2);
      for(j=1;j<=7;j+=2)
        pawn2[j]-=48;
      for(i=0;i<7;i+=2)
        pawn2[i]-=(cg-1)*64;
    }

  }

  cleardevice();
  disp_Struct(pawn,pawn2,a,val);

  if(ch1==24||ch1==67||ch1==88||ch1==99||ch1==72||ch1==39)
  {
    Ladder_Snake_func(&ch1,pawn,1);
    ch=ch1%10;
    cleardevice();
    disp_Struct(pawn,pawn2,a,val);
  }

  else  if(cg1==24||cg1==67||cg1==88||cg1==99||cg1==72||cg1==39)
  {
    Ladder_Snake_func(&cg1,pawn2,2);
    cg=cg1%10;
    cleardevice();
    disp_Struct(pawn,pawn2,a,val);
  }

  k++;
 }

 getch();
 closegraph();

}
```

APPENDIX-II

C++ KEYWORDS

Keywords are reserved to the compiler for use by the language. You cannot define classes, variables, or functions that have these keywords as their names. The list is a bit arbitrary, as some of the keywords are specific to a given compiler.

Auto	delete	goto	register	throw
break	do	if	return	typedef
case	double	int	short	union
catch	else	long	signed	unsigned
char	enum	mutable	sizeof	virtual
class	extern	new	static	void
const	float	operator	struct	volatile
continue	for	private	switch	while
default	friend	protected	template	
		public	this	

ASCII Characters set

The standard ASCII table defines 128 character codes (from 0 to 127), of which, the first 32 are control codes (non-printable), and the remaining 96 character codes are representable characters:

*	0	1	2	3	4	5	6	7	8	9	A	B	C	D	E	F
0	NUL	SOH	STX	ETX	EOT	ENQ	ACK	BEL	BS	TAB	LF	VT	FF	CR	SO	SI
1	DLE	DC1	DC2	DC3	DC4	NAK	SYN	ETB	CAN	EM	SUB	ESC	FS	GS	RS	US
2		!	"	#	$	%	&	'	(	)	*	+	,	-	.	/
3	0	1	2	3	4	5	6	7	8	9	:	;	<	=	>	?
4	@	A	B	C	D	E	F	G	H	I	J	K	L	M	N	O
5	P	Q	R	S	T	U	V	W	X	Y	Z	[	\	]	^	_
6	`	a	b	c	d	e	f	g	h	i	j	k	l	m	n	o
7	p	q	r	s	t	u	v	w	x	y	z	{	|	}	~	

INDEX

F

G

H

I

J

L

M

N

O

P

R